DETOURS

DETOURS

a novel

by

SHIRLEY BAHLMANN

This is a work of fiction, and the views expressed herein are the sole responsibility of the author. Likewise, characters, places, and incidents are either the product of the author's imagination or are represented fictitiously, and any resemblance to actual persons, living or dead, or actual events or locales, is entirely coincidental.

Detours

Published by

CreateSpace

Copyright © 2009 by Shirley Bahlmann

ISBN 978-1448607143

Printed in the United States of America
Year of first printing: 2009

10 9 8 7 6 5 4 3 2 1

DEDICATION

This one's for my oldest son, Andy, who's spent the most time teaching me (with great patience) that there is life after careening crazily down the path and repeatedly falling off the edge.

Thanks for the hugs, son.

Acknowledgements

A huge and heartfelt thank you to Larry Henrikson, who, in his creative wisdom, suggested I take more time to fully develop all the characters. Larry, you were so right! His wife, Gayelene, gave a hearty second to his suggestion.

Other amazing proofreaders were C.L. Beck, Jennie Mickelson, Val Sorenson, Lannette Nielson, Britain Larsen, Greg Anderson, Darla Nielson and her daughter, Kirsten.

Thanks to Zackary Bahlmann for telling me the original first chapter was boring.

Thanks to my Storymaker family for understanding.

Finally, thanks to Father in Heaven for my ten tapping, typing fingers.

CHAPTER 1

A heavy weight hit my back, folding me nearly in half. I staggered, but managed to stay on my feet. Arms slid over my shoulders and wrapped themselves around my neck. "Come with me," a husky voice said close to my ear.

"No!" I screamed, throwing my shoulders back, trying to shake off the unwanted burden.

"It's the only way," the voice murmured in soft tones that chipped at my resolve and sapped my courage. I tried to straighten up, but the arms held tight. Weary from the days' fighting, I stood trembling, slightly off balance.

"It will be so much easier." The unhurried voice was almost soothing.

I closed my eyes. Wouldn't it be wonderful if things were like they'd been before? No fighting, no heart hurting from all of the enemies being people I loved.

"Get away from her," a deep voice commanded. I looked up to see Alex striding toward us, his hair surrounding his head like a dark halo. Curly bangs nearly reached his brown eyes, which were narrowed with intense concentration.

"She hasn't asked me to leave," the voice behind me said. Slow fingers caressed my neck, soothing me with their light touch. I shivered. "She's thinking."

"She doesn't need to think any more!" Alex warned. He stopped right in front of me, standing nearly a head taller. I couldn't see his face very well unless I looked up, and that was uncomfortable because of the arms around my neck. I could see Alex's fists, though, hanging down at his sides. "Casey already made her choice."

"It's not too late to change her mind," the voice said. The words seemed to echo around in my head. ". . . not too late . . . not too late . . ."

"Casey," Alex said, his voice urgent.

"Hm?" seemed to be all I could make myself say.

"Come on, Casey, take my hand." Alex uncurled his fist and stretched out his fingers. His hand was a strong and familiar because I'd held it many times. I slowly lifted my hand, reaching for his.

"No, no, no!" the voice behind me pleaded. "Come with me, Casey. I love you."

Tears filled my eyes, blurring the image of Alex's hand. Maybe the one clinging to my back could be saved. It seemed so helpless, so needy for companionship.

Alex extended across the distance and wrapped his warm hand around mine.

"Come with us," I murmured to the one on my back.

"No!" The voice was loud enough to make me jump. "That way is too risky!" The fingers lovingly traced patterns on my neck. "This way is sure, a promised return. Safety. Easy. Come with me, Casey." The fingers stroked a little faster. "Please."

I blinked my tears away, and there was Alex, his face full of concern, his eyes full of fear. I waited for him to say something, to plead with me, but instead, he relaxed. He didn't let go of my hand, but gave me a gentle smile that warmed me all the way through. All of a sudden, I could see clearly, as though his smile had broken through a gauzy veil that I hadn't known was in front of my eyes. Instantly infused with love and light, I stood up straight. "Leave me," I commanded, giving my shoulders a shake.

"No, Casey, no, don't make me go," the voice behind me was heartbreaking, but I knew it was not sincere. Arms loosened, slipping from my neck.

"Do not come back," I said, my voice firm.

The fingers grasped at my shoulders, then slid off. "You'll be sorry," the voice hissed. I shivered at the malice behind the words.

"You'll be very sorry." Footsteps sounded behind me, quieter and quieter as my attacker moved away. I didn't look back, not even when the distant voice gave a final anguished scream, "Caaasssseeey!" Then it was gone. I knew it was gone because I felt a frightening emptiness in my soul.

"Are you all right?" Alex asked, putting an arm around me.

I nodded, tears pooling in my eyes.

"What's going on?" a female voice called. I blinked back tears to see a beautiful woman with pale skin and silky red hair move in to stand by Alex. Although she was taller than me, she didn't match Alex's height. "Was it another one?"

Alex nodded.

The woman's blue eyes shifted to the expanse behind me. She kept her chin up, and there were no tears in her eyes. "It's hard for all of us, Casey," she said. "We loved the ones that left, too."

"I know," I sighed.

Megan had been one of the staunchest defenders of Father's plan, standing before His children and calling to us in her firm voice. Now she leaned in and gave me a hug almost hard enough to hurt. The emptiness of the lost loved one closed a bit at her embrace.

A petite young woman with shining dark hair hurried toward us, tears streaming down her cheeks. "They're all gone!" she wailed. "Why wouldn't they stay?" She burrowed her face into my shoulder.

"Sh, sh, Kim, it will be all right," I murmured through my own tears. "They chose their way, we chose ours." We stood together, crying, until a light footstep sounded on the path.

"Hey, who died?" a voice called.

I wiped tears away and saw Derrick's blue eyes dancing with mischief. "No one," I answered. "We haven't even been born yet, so how can we die?"

"Exactly," Derrick said, standing with his feet apart and his hands on his hips. "So let's go on this Earth journey. We've all got tickets, right?"

Kim's head lifted, her panicked eyes staring through wet eyelashes. "I don't have a ticket."

"Sure you do," Derrick said. "Every one of us gets to go to

Earth. That's the ticket! It's invisible." He rubbed his hands together. "I can hardly wait! This is going to be fun!"

"I don't know what it will be like," Kim said. She pressed her palms over her eyes. "I'm scared."

"Don't worry, I'll go with you," I said.

Kim looked up at me. "You really will?"

"Sure," I answered, giving her shoulders a squeeze.

"Me, too," Megan chimed in.

"Hey, don't leave me out," Alex said.

"Well, you seem like a fun group, I'll just tag along with you guys," Derrick said. "Are we ready?"

I gave him a woeful grin. "Ready or not, here we come."

CHAPTER 2

Someone gently kicked my foot. I gave a start and opened my eyes to find myself in a warm, puffy sleeping bag on lush green grass. The sun wasn't up yet, but it colored the sky in impossibly beautiful orange and vanilla ice cream swirls with violet edges.

"Time to go," a man standing over me said with far too much glee for so early in the morning. A playful breeze trailed the scent of honeysuckle across my face. I sat up, running a hand through my tousled brown hair, eyes focused on his hiking boots. Then I quickly scanned past his blue jeans and red shirt to see chestnut hair curled against the collar of a plaid shirt spanning his broad shoulders. But it was his eyes that made me forgive him, even though he had to be the foot kicker. I couldn't help but like the humor I saw there. He extended a hand to help me up, I took hold, and he pulled me to my feet.

I looked around the grassy hilltop where we stood cradled by trees in a horseshoe shape, like green leafy arms holding us close. Each tree was heavy with new growth, the subtle scent of greenery riding the breeze. Several bushes at the edge of the meadow beamed with bright yellow blossoms. Beside them, pink wild rose branches tangled themselves in the soft breeze. I grinned like I was at my own birthday party.

Then I discovered another scent.

Food.

My stomach rumbled when I saw a picnic table set under a shelter with several people gathered around a camp stove. I also caught sight of the corner of a small cinderblock building, which turned out to be a restroom and my first destination.

When I came out, the delicious smell of browning pancakes kicked my hunger into high gear. I headed toward the table and the thick, sweet smell of hot maple syrup. A few flies had the same idea. I reached out to swish them away, but a large muscled arm beat me to it, somersaulting the flies out into the trees. I looked up to see Alex smiling down at me. He was dressed in a navy T-shirt and blue jeans. Blue and white cushioned running shoes covered his huge feet. "Alex!" I cried.

"Hey, Casey," he said in his deep voice. "You hungry?"

"Starving," I answered.

"I already ate," Alex said, extending his hand toward a picnic table. "You can have my spot."

"Thanks," I said.

I turned toward the table and nearly ran over Kim, standing by the cook stove in a light blue warm up suit. Sleek black hair skimmed her shoulders and fell forward as she peered into the pancake pan, a spatula raised in one of her hands like a flag of surrender.

"Kim!" I yelled. "Is one of those for me?"

I must have startled her, because she jumped. Her black eyes darted up to mine, then grew as wide as her smile. "Hey, Casey! You woke up! Sorry we didn't wait for you to eat. It's just that we were all so hungry."

"That's okay," I said.

Kim's face grew serious. "I heard that this journey may be harder than we thought."

"It'll be all right," I assured her. "I'll be ready to go as soon as I eat." The sharp odor of scorched food drifted past my nose. "The pancake . . ."

"Oh, oh, oh, the pancake!" Kim interrupted, flailing her spatula around in the air before stabbing it beneath the smoking circle of batter. When she flipped it over, half the pancake flopped over the edge of the pan, black side up. Kim flapped her hands, stirring smoke around in the air. "I don't understand," Kim cried. "I never burned anything before!"

"Move over, Kim, let me help." Megan slid into Kim's spot

and expertly flipped the burned pancake from the pan, her red ponytail swishing. Then she looked down at me with incredibly clear green eyes, her pale, butter yellow sweatshirt accenting milky white skin.

I suddenly felt a twisting inside, a strange and uncomfortable sensation right at chest level. I didn't like it, but didn't know how to make it go away, either. I ruffled a hand through my brown hair, suddenly wishing it were long and silky. I yearned for smooth white skin, and desperately wanted to be taller. But I wasn't. And because I wasn't, I resented Megan for being all those things.

"Now then, Casey, how many would you like?" Megan asked, her brisk voice grating on my nerves even though she spoke with a smile.

"A couple of dozen," I muttered.

Megan poured the batter, which soon bubbled up into a pale puff. "Sit down," Megan said. "I'll bring them to you." She stared at the pancake, daring it to burn, her spatula poised like a threat at the edge of the pan.

Some guy sat at the picnic table, showing me the back expanse of his floppy Hawaiian shirt. As soon as I climbed onto the bench beside him, he turned his freckled face and met my gaze with crossed blue eyes. "Hey, Derrick!" I said, giving him a playful punch on the shoulder. He grinned and reached an arm around to pull me in for a hug. The next thing I knew, his other hand darted out and streaked sticky syrup on my nose.

"Hey!" I pulled away and grabbed a napkin to dab off the goo.

"Sweets for the sweet," Derrick said. His grin was irresistible. I smiled back, even though I didn't appreciate him putting fly bait on me.

"Here you go." Megan dropped two large perfectly tanned pancakes onto my plate. "There are a dozen bites in each one," she said. "That makes two dozen, as ordered."

"Thanks," I said, my stomach rumbling in delight, apparently as grateful as I was that the jealous feelings had slipped away.

"As soon as you're done, we'll go," Megan said.

Kim shuffled over to the table as I spread butter and poured a generous portion of shining dark syrup. One of Kim's hands was weighed down with a plate of fresh, golden pineapple circles. A bowl of bright red strawberries tipped in her other hand. "Which one do you want?" she asked, just as I took a warm, buttery bite.

"What about bananas?" Derrick asked. "Why don't you offer her bananas?"

"Because you ate the last one," Kim answered.

"Oh." Derrick looked at me with guilty eyes. "I'm sorry."

I swallowed and said, "It's okay. I'd rather eat pineapple."

"You're just saying that," Derrick answered.

"No," I insisted. "If you peeled a banana and shoved it in my face, I'd keep my lips closed."

"No you wouldn't."

"I would."

"Then I'd have to feed you banana through your nose."

"Derrick!" I yelped.

"Lucky we're all out," he said, waggling his eyebrows.

"Set those bowls down before your arms fall off," I said to Kim. She plunked the bowls down on the table.

"Thanks," I said.

"Hey, Kim, do you mind giving me a hand? Grab the broom, will you?" Megan asked. Kim turned toward Megan and I took another bite.

"How about you, Derrick?" Megan called. "You up for a little dustpan work?"

"Uh . . . I think I forgot to roll up my sleeping bag," Derrick said.

Strong hands descended onto my shoulders. I looked up into Alex's face, a little surprised that he was just as handsome upside down as he was right side up. "We're gathering supplies for the journey," he said. "As soon as you're done, meet us by the path." He gestured toward a dark path running through the grass a few yards away.

I nodded and chewed faster.

CHAPTER 3

After ruffling my hair, Derrick bounded away to join Alex. Megan and Kim cleaned up in amiable silence as I finished my food. When I stood, I saw Kim bent over one leg in a practiced runner's stretch. "All done?" she asked.

I nodded, then moved closer to the path. It looked like the spongy kind of blacktop, the delight of runners and dedicated walkers. This would be an easy journey.

Megan moved in to stand beside me. "So, Sleeping Beauty, are you ready to go?"

"I'm sorry if I kept you waiting," I said.

When Megan nodded, her ponytail swayed gently. "Everyone has their own degree of self motivation." She stretched her arms over her head with interlocked fingers. "Yesterday was a big day for you." She tipped her torso to the right. "Today will be even bigger."

"I'm ready," I said, my chin rising in an unfamiliar gesture of defiance. "I can handle it."

"Just remember, I'm always willing to help when you need me," Megan said, staring at me. After a long moment, I reluctantly nodded. Megan was only offering to help, but I was annoyed that she assumed I'd need it.

"Come on, you girls," Derrick called. I looked up to see him standing by Alex and our host. "Let's get going."

"You're right," I said. "We have places to go and things to see."

Kim took my arm on one side and Megan linked her arm with

mine on the other. "We're off to have adventures," they said, twirling me around. I laughed and pulled free, staggering a little from dizziness. All seemed right again.

The man in jeans and hiking boots smiled and beckoned for us to come closer. Then he said, "There are others waiting to take this journey."

Kim's eyes went round. "You mean we're the first ones?"

"Others have gone before you," he said, "and others will follow." He swept his arm around the landscape. When I turned to look, I saw several other picnic tables serving as gathering places for groups of people spread around the grassy area. It was odd that I hadn't noticed them before, but none of the people seemed to notice us, either. No one looked our way as they cooked, ate, and talked together.

"Now is your time to go," said our host.

I turned around, tucking in my shirt. "I'll go anywhere with my friends."

"Each of you will begin your journey alone," our host said, "but later you may choose to travel with one another or continue by yourself. Let us begin."

A sudden, embarrassing realization hit me. I wondered if I should ask the question that popped into my mind. I darted glances at my fellow travelers, who were darting glances back at me. Was I the only one who didn't know? No one else opened their mouths, and I really wanted to understand, so I finally took a deep breath and blurted, "Um . . . could you please remind me where we're going?"

"I'll show you," he said.

"I feel kind of silly that I don't remember," I admitted.

"Don't worry, it happens to everyone," he said. "Just be sure you remember the warning."

I squinted my eyes, thinking. "Is that the one about we need to travel to the best of our ability to get a reward?"

"And . . ." he prompted.

I frowned, searching my mind. "Oh, yes." I raised a triumphant gaze to his. "It will be easier if we follow the signs."

"Good," he said. "That's right. Now follow me." He led the way to the center of the path, and we all followed him. When I stepped on the blacktop, I was delighted to discover that I was right about it being firm, yet slightly yielding to the pressure of my sneakers. My eyes followed the trail to where it curved down out of sight into a green valley. "Your destination is there," our host said, pointing toward a far hillside.

Although appearing as a pencil stroke from where I stood, by squinting I could make out the distant path curving up and out from a stand of trees. "Here, these might help," our host said, pressing a pair of binoculars into my hand. When I lifted them to my eyes, the path leapt closer. The smudged spots of color on either side turned into bright flowers waiting for the morning sun to coax them awake. My gaze didn't linger on the flowers, but followed the road as it crossed a gentle slope and rolled itself under an ornate metal gate set in a fence of golden slats. Sparkling through the slats was the undulating gleam of a working fountain. I was too far away to hear the music of dancing water, but I fancied that I could almost catch the cooling rhythm. Peering through the fence slats, it appeared that the trail zigzagged through lush green trees, leading the way to a breathtaking mansion, vast and ornate, with balconies, turrets, porches, patios, and interesting eyebrow windows set in the roof.

At that very moment, the sun broke free of the horizon, shooting its light over everything. The fountain sprayed diamonds and the fence slats shone like golden mirrors. The wonderful house reveled in the fresh sunlight. I suddenly longed to be there as much as I longed for food after a three-day fast.

"Wow," said Kim. "Where do I sign up for a tour?"

"What tour?" said Megan. "I want to live there."

"I want to play golf on those lawns," said Derrick, looking through his own pair of binoculars. "There's not a blemish on them."

"I want to eat," said Alex.

"There will be food for you once you arrive," said our host.

I lowered the binoculars and gauged the distance with my eyes. I could be there by lunchtime. Easy.

Everyone lowered their binoculars while our host continued. "All you need to do is follow the trail. There are sign posts along the way that will help you if you follow the directions."

I glanced up at him to see his intense gaze fixed on me. As soon as our eyes locked, comforting warmth slid from my head to my feet as though I'd been planted in the center of a warm sunbeam after a cold shower. He blessed me with a smile that made my skin tingle.

Breaking eye contact, he turned to a pile of colorful backpacks stacked beside the trail. Lifting a yellow one and a green one in each hand, he handed them to Derrick and me. "What's this?" Derrick asked, holding his pack up in his left hand and poking the bright yellow fabric with his right index finger.

"It's your lunch, along with a few other odds and ends you might find useful." Our host picked up two more packs, handing the red one to Megan and the cream colored one to Kim.

"I probably won't need it," I said, hanging the pack from one finger, dangerously close to dropping it. I glanced over to the mansion across the valley. "I can make it by lunchtime."

Our host handed the final pack, a navy blue one, to Alex. "It's up to you whether you take it or not," he said. "I think you might find it useful. It doesn't weigh much, and it's waterproof."

I glanced up at the blue sky. What possible difference could it make if the packs were waterproof? But one thing he was right about was that it didn't weigh much, so it shouldn't slow me down any. I made a decision and hoisted the pack onto my back, slipping my arms through the shoulder straps. There was probably water in there, and I could stand to take a swig or two before I reached the wondrous estate. I hoped there would be lunch when I got there, something nicer than a smashed sandwich and a crumbling cupcake. I mean, what kind of reward would it be if there were nothing good to eat? I adjusted the pack and glanced across the valley again. I was ready to go.

Derrick was ahead of me in line. Our host walked up to him and said, "Derrick, are you ready?" Derrick nodded, still wearing his smile, which was as permanent a fixture on his face as his freckles. "Then go, and remember to heed the signs," our host said. He pulled Derrick into a brief hug, then let him go. Derrick headed down the trail at a jaunty pace.

I was next. Our host looked me in the eye, and it was as though he were looking clear through me, all the way down to my toes.

Yet, strangely enough, I didn't mind. My trust in him was absolute.

"Are you ready?" he asked.

I nodded, eager to be on my way.

"Heed the signs," he said.

There was something in his voice that made the hair on my arms and legs tingle, something that was so deeply significant that it nearly made me tremble, but not with fear. With intensity. The man who had teased me awake was deeply concerned with my welfare. I knew for certain that he wanted me to have a good journey, and he really wanted me to obey the signs. I wondered what the signs might be. I knew of emergency exit signs, road signs, and men at work signs. But what kind of signs could possibly make any difference on this short trail? I saw my destination well enough that I could almost make it there with my eyes closed.

He was waiting.

"All right," I said.

His smile was so warm and loving that my heart could hardly contain it all. Without a doubt, he cherished a deep desire for me to reach that gorgeous estate. After wrapping his arms around me for a brief embrace, he sent me off down the trail.

Infused with energy, I started down the path with a light step. Soon I saw Derrick's backpack bobbing up and down, up and down, as he hurried along the road. I enjoyed the feel of soft pavement beneath my shoes. I didn't even look back when I heard our host address Megan.

Derrick's legs were longer than mine, but it didn't bother me. He was still in sight, and if I called to him, I was sure he'd wait. But I saw no reason to slow him down just now.

Suddenly, Derrick stopped at the bottom of the hill. His head went one way, and then the other. He appeared to be puzzled. Drawing closer, I saw the black path level out and disappear under a lush canopy of green leaves where flowers lined the path. Blue bunches of forget-me-nots, like berries spilled from a pail, scattered along the edge of the grass. Bright birds fluttered among the branches, twittering an occasional measure of song. At first I couldn't figure out why Derrick had stopped instead of moving into the inviting shade. I kept walking, wondering if he was waiting for me so we could walk together.

When I caught up to him, I saw that it wasn't me who had the power to stop him. It was the "Detour" sign we faced. It was certainly an odd place for one, as I saw nothing wrong with the smooth path ahead. By contrast, I saw a lot wrong with the rutted road the thick black "Detour" arrow pointed down. It curved to the right, into a patch of tangled undergrowth that huddled beneath a thick stand of dark, foreboding trees. The trail may have been used once a long time ago, but only by a herd of wayward cows.

I couldn't figure it out. Detours were generally used for well-traveled roads in need of repair, but the path the sign wanted us to leave looked brand new. If our host hadn't said otherwise, I could have believed we were the first travelers to ever walk on it.

Derrick scratched his head. "That's odd."

"It certainly is," I said.

"Well," Derrick said, "I don't see why we can't just continue on."

"Because there's a "Detour" sign," I said, pointing.

"I see that," Derrick said, flashing me a grin. "But, come on, Casey, the path we're on obviously leads to the estate, while that one," he pointed to the dirt track, "veers off to the boondocks."

"But we were told to follow the signs," I reminded him.

"How do we know who put this here?" Derrick jabbed a thumb toward the sign. "Maybe someone set it up to play a trick on us."

I stepped forward, put my hand on the sign, and tried to wiggle it. It was set solidly in the ground. I looked back at Derrick and raised my shoulders. "Who else is around?"

"The ones who went before us," Derrick said. "They could be hiding anywhere. Maybe they're watching us right now, laughing at the prank they played." When he fell silent, I glanced at the shadows underneath the trees, but didn't see anyone. Derrick continued, "Maybe it's someone from the estate." He planted his hands on his hips and stared across the valley as though he might catch someone dodging from tree trunk to tree trunk.

"Hey, what are you doing?" Megan asked as she came up behind us.

"Deciding which way to go," I said.

Megan surveyed the situation. "What is there to decide?" she asked. "I'm following the sign."

"What if it's the wrong way?" Derrick wanted to know.

Megan hitched up the straps of her pack. "I can always come back."

"Then I'll get there before you," Derrick said, sidestepping the "Detour" sign.

Megan stared at him. "You're supposed to follow the signs."

"Only the ones that make sense," Derrick said. Then he turned and strode down the paved path.

My stomach clenched. "Derrick!" I called.

He turned to give me one of his irrepressible grins and a cheerful wave. "It's all right," he said. "Come with me, Casey. It'll be fun!" His hand turned over, palm up, and he curled his fingers in a beckoning gesture while continuing slowly down the path.

"Follow the signs, Casey," Megan said, then headed down the dirt track with just as much determination.

I stood at the junction of the two paths, glancing from Derrick to Megan and back again.

"Hey, what's going on?" Kim asked as she stopped beside me.

"I'm deciding which way to go," I said.

Kim looked after Derrick, who was growing both smaller and shorter as he walked away down the incline from us. Then she turned to see Megan disappear behind a stand of scruffy trees further along the dirt trail.

"Oh, no," Kim said, crinkling her brow. "Who's right? Which way should I go?"

She sidled over to the edge of the trail and sat on a bench I hadn't noticed until now. It was made of smooth, carved wood, and looked comfortable. It rested beneath a large tree with leaves that murmured soothingly to whoever sat in their shade.

Kim leaned back against the contours of the bench. "I'm just going to sit here and think about it for a minute." Her eyes closed, and her worried brow smoothed.

I looked at the sign one more time. It still said, "Detour." The arrow still insisted on the dirt path. I remembered the intensity in our host's eyes. I glanced back along the path I'd already traveled and saw Alex walking toward me, his face eager, but there was no sign of our host. He wasn't with us anymore, at least, nowhere I could see.

But his last bit of advice echoed in my head.

Heed the signs.

I sighed, hitched up my pack, and turned toward the uneven dirt road. "See you later, Kim," I said, and started down the dirt track. Before I was out of hearing range, I heard Alex ask, "What's going on?" and Kim's quiet reply, "I'm deciding which way to go."

CHAPTER 4

I pushed on through the thick branches, getting another one in my face while several clawed at my legs. How could Megan walk so fast through this thicket? A brief fear brushed my mind. Maybe I'd missed her. She said she'd turn back if this was the wrong way, but how could I have failed to notice if she had turned around? There was no way through this thicket that I could see except the narrow dirt trail under my feet. The thought of stepping off the path scared me, and not just because of the thick woods. Thin, sadistic branches delighted in whipping flesh even while on the trail, so before anyone ever found their way out, they'd likely become so hopelessly tangled that they'd petrify into a tree themselves.

Then I spied a flash of red moving up ahead. "Megan?" I called.

There was a pause, then Megan's voice drifted back to me. "Yeah? Casey?"

"It's me," I called.

Megan laughed. "Decided to follow the primrose path?"

"Yeah, I did," I replied. "That was before I remembered that roses have thorns." Now I was right behind Megan and saw her face turned back to look at me. I gasped in horror at the red welt slashed across one of her cheeks. "Oh, wow, what happened to you?" I asked.

"Which time?"

"Your face, it's like you got whipped," I said.

Megan grinned. "Which time?" she repeated. Her eyes scanned

my face. "You've got extra rosy cheeks yourself. These branches are no respecter of faces. Let's push on."

The trail was too narrow for us to move side by side, so I followed behind Megan. Traveling through the trees was easier with her ahead of me. After walking a few yards, I asked, "Do you think Derrick's okay?"

"As okay as he can be, considering he took the wrong path," Megan answered.

"It looked like it led to the estate," I said. "Maybe it's just another way to get there."

"And I think if he wants to get to the estate, he'll have to back track and follow the "Detour" sign," Megan said. "Haven't you ever done those mazes where you follow a line that looks like it will take you straight to 'finish'?"

"Yes."

"And how many times does the shortest path work?"

"Never."

Megan nodded. "It's usually the longest, most looping trail that eventually gets you through the maze."

What she said made sense. Then I thought of something else. "Do you think Derrick will be allowed to go back?"

"I didn't see any fences," Megan answered. "It looks like we can go wherever we want."

"Except off this trail," I said, sidestepping to avoid another branch in my face.

"I think it's thinning out," Megan said.

I craned my neck, trying to see ahead of her. I had to agree that the trees seemed further apart, and the undergrowth was less dense. I took a deep, grateful breath. It felt as though we were being released from prison. Soon the trees gave way altogether, turning us loose onto a beach covered with sand the color of golden coins. It was so startling that I stood and stared, taking in the welcome sight of blueberry waves tasting the sand.

"Wow," said Megan. A gentle breeze brushed a strand of red hair across her face, camouflaging the welt. "Now this was worth the walk."

I had to agree. I pressed my toes against the heels of my sneakers and stepped out of my shoes. Then I bent and yanked off my socks. The soft sand, as fine as flour and completely free of shells or rocks, cooled my toes.

"Good idea," Megan said. She took off her shoes and socks. Then we moved together toward the beach, scooting our feet through the soft grains, feeling the tickle of them trailing between our toes. When we reached the water's edge, I looked out over the sparkling blue water undulating into shore. "Those aren't very big waves," I said.

"It's a lake," Megan answered, pointing across the expanse of blue. My gaze followed her finger and I spied a far shore. Dipping my toes into the water, I drew in a big lungful of moist air, savoring it before I let it out.

"Look, there's something over there," Megan said, pointing with her slender arm. A few yards away stood a wooden board nailed to a signpost sticking out of the sand at the water's edge. Megan walked toward it, leaving bare footprints in the yellow sand while I splashed beside her through ankle deep water. When we were close enough to see the writing, we read a single word. "Swim."

"Swim?" I asked, pulling back in disbelief. "Is this for real?"

"How else will we get across?" Megan asked.

I shook my head. "I don't know. Maybe we could walk around?"

"Do you know how big this lake is?"

"No."

"Can you see the other shore from here?"

"Yes."

"And what does the sign say?"

"I can read the sign," I said, resentment rising up in my chest like a hard stone. I folded my arms across my chest. "What are we supposed to do, swim in our clothes?"

"I don't think so." Megan shrugged off her backpack and unzipped it. She fished around inside for a minute, then pulled out a small red piece of fabric and held it up.

"What's that?" I asked.

"A swimming suit," Megan said. She turned around and pointed to a couple of small white wooden booths sitting a few yards back from shore. "And there are the changing rooms. I'll race ya!" Megan took off at a run for the nearest changing booth, ducking inside and closing the door behind her.

I yanked off my pack. Before it settled into the sand, I was rummaging inside. In just moments I came up with a swimming suit of emerald green. Holding it in one hand, I picked up my pack with the other and headed for the second changing booth, slamming the door behind me so Megan would know I was in the running. But by the time I got into my suit and opened the door, Megan was already in the water, swimming several yards out from shore with her backpack riding behind her like a misshapen red rubber duckie.

"Hey!" I called.

Megan turned over so she could see me, treading water and sculling with her hands. "Water's fine," she called. "Come on in."

Suddenly filled with apprehension, I stood and stared at Megan, not knowing if I was a good enough swimmer to get all the way across the lake.

"Remember, your pack's waterproof," Megan called, her voice both friendly and encouraging. Then she rolled onto her stomach, her backpack perched jauntily on her shoulders, and knifed through the water with sure strokes.

"Megan!" I called, repenting of any earlier ill feeling toward her. "Wait for me!" Whether she didn't hear or simply chose to ignore me, she kept on going.

I couldn't even pretend I was as good a swimmer as Megan. I was only really good at the sidestroke and dog paddle, with a resting backstroke that pretty much consisted of flutter-kicking my feet and weaving my hands in and out to keep my head above water. "You can make it," I muttered to myself. "You can make it." I willed myself to believe it, then lifted my pack and slipped it over my shoulders. It was heavier with my clothes and shoes inside. I strode out into the lake, pushing confidently against the force of water until it was above my knees. Then I stopped suddenly, water swirling around my legs, sucking at my flesh as though eager to swallow the rest of me. The sudden sickening thought filled my head that "waterproof" didn't always mean "buoyant." Sealed cans were waterproof, some lead boxes were waterproof, but they didn't float. Lots of sea chests and steamer trunks were found in shipwrecks on the bottom of the ocean. Megan's pack looked like it floated, but maybe she just made it look that way because she was such a good swimmer.

I hurried back to the beach, splashing my way through water that tried to drag me back. I stood on the shore and gazed out across the lake once more, the air curiously cold against my dripping legs but warm on my dry arms. I could see a rather small Megan in the distance, still swimming strong.

I sighed and put my hand on top of the "Swim" sign. It was unexpectedly sturdy in its foothold of sand. Well, I thought. Megan's on top of the water, so it's likely that I will be, too. I certainly didn't want to stand here for the rest of my life, and I wasn't going back. With an infusion of fresh courage, I returned to the water, wading in up to my knees, then my hips. The next thing I knew, cool blue lake water licked at my waist while my heart beat hard enough to create a tidal wave.

This was taking too long. I decided to test the pack now, while I could still touch bottom. Before I could talk myself out of it, I ducked under the waves. The pack strained against my shoulders toward the surface. My face bobbed back above the water, grinning, and I began to kick my way across the lake.

CHAPTER 5

When my arms tired, I stopped to check my progress. The shore I wanted to reach looked just as distant as when I'd begun. Treading water, I searched the lake surface, my breath coming in gasps, but I couldn't see Megan anywhere. Even though I hadn't really expected to find her, my heart grew heavy with disappointment. She was probably on the far shore already, on solid ground, and I was envious. Even though my backpack would keep me suspended indefinitely, I longed for a solid place to rest. Where would I find such a place in the middle of a lake?

I slowly paddled my hands, turning slowly in the blue water until I faced the way I'd come. At least the beach behind me appeared to be as far away as the shore I was aiming for.

I turned over onto my back and rested my head against my buoyant pack, letting my arms and legs hang suspended in the cool water. I was weightless. My breathing slowed as my eyes closed, blocking off the discouraging sight of distant land. This wasn't a race. At least I didn't think it was. The only part that was clear in my mind was that if we finished our journey, we would get a reward. I lazily searched my memory, but didn't find anything about the first one there being the grand prize winner, and anyone else straggling in being losers. I would like to get there soon, though. I was getting hungry.

I wondered if Derrick was already there, within the shining gates of the estate, drinking cold lemonade and eating something yummy on one of the many patios around the mansion. I imagined him looking out over the valley he'd traveled on that smooth blacktop, enjoying the shade, hearing birdsong as he ambled along. And here I was, hanging in the water, worn out from swimming. Not only that, I'd been in the water so long my skin was wrinkling.

My brow creased at the unfairness of it all, until I imagined a songbird's egg falling on Derrick's head with a satisfying splat, followed by egg goo running into his eyes.

I wiped the dreamy smile off my face. Enough of that. Derrick had chosen his path and I had chosen mine. I made myself roll onto my stomach, preparing to paddle onward. That's when I noticed a skinny rock ledge surprisingly near. How could I have missed it before? Maybe a current had pulled me to this rocky outcrop while I was daydreaming. Whatever the reason, I found the sight of land, no matter how narrow, delightful. Here was a real resting place, a spot I could maybe dry out and un-wrinkle before finishing my swim.

But as I drew closer, I saw that this place wasn't much of an improvement over my pack, since the rock outcrop offered no sandy beach. In fact, as I looked it over more carefully, I couldn't even see a flat place to crawl onto. There was just a steep rock wall pocked with ledges that balanced different sized boulders in precarious positions overhead. Was it safe enough for me to move closer?

The decision was made for me when I spied a single narrow stone shelf at water level, edging out a little way before blending back into the rock. To my eyes, it was decidedly better than nothing. I windmilled and kicked until I came close enough to glide in and grab hold of the ledge. It felt good to get a solid grip on something. The only problem was that my resting place was below a couple of boulders balanced on ridiculously small ledges. I hoped they'd stay put long enough for me to rest.

My breathing had just become slow and even when I was startled by a voice calling, "My dog swims better than you." Heart thumping, I glanced up to see a boy of about twelve standing on top of the cliff. I squinted at him. His wavy blonde hair was cut above his ears with one stubborn piece sticking up on the side of his head. He had a straight nose and soft gray eyes that slanted slightly upward as he showed me a mischievous grin. Where had he come from? I certainly hadn't seen him when I'd looked for a handhold. But there he was.

After a few seconds to regain my composure and get used to the idea of someone else being in a place I thought was deserted, I answered, "Well, your dog's not here, is he? So I guess I win."

"You're not going to win anything," the boy shouted.

His unexpected words kindled worry in my soul. Had I missed part of the orientation? What had our host told the others while I was asleep? Was this journey really a contest? The first one wins, the other four get absolutely nothing? What did this boy know that I didn't?

"Have you been messing with the signs?" I asked suddenly.

"Signs?" the boy raised his eyebrows, which opened his eyes up into round circles of virtue. "What signs?" His innocence was so badly feigned that I wanted to lasso him and drag him into the lake. If there hadn't been such a sheer expanse of rock between us, I might have tried climbing up so I could make him answer my questions.

"You know what signs," I said.

The boy didn't admit to anything. Instead, he picked up a walnut-sized rock from the ground and tossed it into the water beside me.

"Hey!" I called out.

"I haven't seen any signs," he said.

"Yeah, right," I shot back.

"Glad you agree." Then he tossed a whole handful of rocks my way.

"Knock it off!" I yelled, dodging to one side.

"I'm trying to," the boy said, sizing me up and bending down to pick up a rock as big as his fist. "But you won't hold still."

Even though I longed to rest a while longer, I had no desire for my head to resemble a chunk of Swiss cheese. I pushed off and stroked toward the far shore just as the boy heaved his rock. Fortunately it missed, but it struck close enough to splash me in the face. "I take back what I said," the boy called. "You don't swim worse than my dog. You swim worse than a mangy, no-tailed cat."

I'd show him. Pulling with long strokes, I dug into the water and swam like I'd never swum before, away from the boy and his taunts, as fast as I could go. I stroked for a while without looking back. At last I checked to make sure I was out of rock-throwing range. I could see the rocky island, but not the boy. The more I looked, the more certain I was that he really was gone, at least from sight. I hoped he headed back to wherever he came from and that we'd never cross paths again.

With the worry of getting hit by a rock behind me, crossing the last stretch of water seemed much easier. I set my sights on the distant shore and headed toward it, huffing and puffing, occasionally getting a mouthful of water for my efforts. I didn't care because I was making real progress now, and feeling rather pleased with myself.

Then I noticed movement off to one side. I turned to see what it was. To my utter astonishment, a trim, white boat glided over the water like a pleasant dream. I couldn't take my eyes off it. My feet kicked so slowly I almost forgot they were there. I hadn't known there was a boat. No one told me. But now that I knew, I wanted a ride.

Then I saw movement on deck. Someone walked along the railing, someone dry who was crossing the lake without struggling to keep their nose above water. Suddenly, I felt so tired that it was hard to summon enough energy to wave my arms to get her attention. Even if I couldn't get on board in the middle of the lake, at least she could throw me a life ring and tow me to shore.

When the passenger didn't respond to my frantic waves, I tried calling, "Hey, over here!" She moved to lean against the railing where a flash of sunlight polished a head of shiny black hair. Kim! I stuck my arm up out of the water again and waved with more energy, calling, "Kim! Over here! Kim!" but she didn't seem to see me. Her gaze was fixed on our destination. The boat glided past, and I was left to swim alone, muttering, "No one told me there was a boat!"

CHAPTER 6

The boat disappeared from sight. I'm not sure where it went, because I was too busy swimming to notice. Finally, I felt damp earth shifting beneath my feet. I scrabbled my toes to find a foothold, then splashed up out of the water onto dry sand. My legs collapsed beneath me like a folding chair bearing too much weight. Breathing was hard. With my cheek pressed against the earth, explosions of air scattered fine grains of sand before me. As the sun dried the lake water from my skin, I relaxed. My breathing slowed, my eyes closed, drifting toward sleep.

Before I shut the world out completely, a buzz sounded in my ear. I flicked an impatient hand at the fly and settled back into my sandy bed. Before long, several annoying tickles on various points of skin let me know that the flies weren't leaving just because I wanted them to.

A splashing sound brought me up to a sitting position. I turned toward the lake and saw Alex swimming into shore with powerful strokes. He pulled himself out of the water, shook himself, and shot me a grin. "Having a bit of a snooze?" He bent over, catching his breath, water dripping from his brow. His breathing was heavy, but he hadn't collapsed like I had. I was a bit put out to be caught resting when Alex seemed ready to go on. Maybe he'd missed the kid on the cliff.

"Hey, Alex, did you run across a blonde kid?"

"What, that little mosquito?" Alex shrugged the pack off his shoulders and bent to unzip it. "Yeah, he tried pelting me, but I threw a couple back at him. When he hit the dirt, I dove under the water and kept on going. Didn't even give the little bozo the satisfaction of an argument."

I wondered if Alex had overheard me arguing with the kid. I hoped not. Alex reached into his pack and pulled out a big, fluffy towel. Did I have one of those? I pulled out my jumbled clothes and, sure enough, a towel surfaced. "I didn't see this before," I said.

Alex rubbed his hair with his towel, then shook his head like a dog just out of the water. His dark hair fell into curls on either side of his face. "Yeah, it seems that you get just what you need," he said. He plunked down on the sand beside me. "And I need to eat." He dug around in his pack and came out with a couple of foil wrapped bars. "You want one?"

"Sure," I said, accepting the food. He pulled back the paper and started to eat. I peeled the foil from one end of my bar and asked, "Did you see Kim on the boat?"

Alex nodded, swallowed, then said somberly, "I feel sorry for her."

"Sorry?" I asked, my eyes wide with surprise. "Why?"

Alex shrugged. "She didn't swim."

"But she got across the lake," I said. "Does it really matter how we got here?"

Alex took another bite and looked back the way we had come, his eyes narrowed in thought. I took a bite of my bar. Although solid, it was wonderfully smooth and creamy with a delicious taste that was not too sweet. I could feel nourishing energy flow into my limbs, replenishing my strength as I chewed.

Alex swallowed, then said, "I think it does. There's a reason for the things we're asked to do."

"But it was so hard," I said, wrapping my arms around my knees. I took another bite.

"It was," Alex agreed. "And now we're here on the other side. How does that make you feel?"

I considered his question. With the lake behind me, sitting on the sand beside Alex was pretty comfortable. I'd swum clear across the lake, even when I wasn't sure I could make it, and now I was safe and fed and nearly dry. "I feel good," I said.

"Me too." Alex grinned. He flexed his arm, and his muscles

hardened. "I think my muscles got bigger. I'd swim this far instead of boating any day. And now I'm ready to go." He popped the rest of his bar into his mouth, then stood and pulled his shirt and trousers on over his swimming suit. "Are you coming?" he asked, holding out a hand in invitation.

"I'm going to change first," I said, gesturing with what remained of my bar toward the changing booths just down the beach.

"Okay," Alex replied. "Take care. See you at the mansion." He shouldered his pack and headed down the trail, following a sign with an arrow marked, "This way."

I ate the rest of my bar as I watched him go. Then I made a fist and curled my arm up and felt my bicep. It felt no bigger than before. I sighed and pushed myself to my feet. Even though I was pretty sure this wasn't a race, Rock Boy had planted doubts in my mind. I'd reached shore before Alex, so I'd expected to hit the trail ahead of him, too. But it was too late for that now. Megan was surely in front of me, and lucky duck boat-riding Kim must be ahead of Alex. I was the last one. I could only hope that there would be something good left for me to eat by the time I reached the estate.

CHAPTER 7

I'd been out of the water long enough for the sun to dry my skin, but I rubbed down with the towel anyway, as much to get the fly-feet feeling off me as anything else. Then I ducked into a room and changed. I left the booth, hoisted my pack on my back, and gave the "This Way" sign a pat as I passed by.

This trail wasn't as rutted as the one that had led into the thicket. It was dirt, but flat, which made it fairly comfortable to walk on. I swung my drying hair from side to side, feeling the weight of it against my neck. After fighting my way through the underbrush at the first detour, I appreciated the elbow room between the trail and the trees on this stretch of road.

Before long, my hair dried completely and feathered around my face. I enjoyed the light tickle of it against my neck as I took long strides. It felt good to be on my feet again. My hair flew over my face, and I pushed it back with one hand, wishing I had a headband or pins to keep it out of my eyes.

That's when I heard a strange noise. For a split second, I thought of a magic genie granting my wish. But that was ridiculous, wasn't it? I froze, listening, puzzled at what sounded like music flowing through the trees. A melodious clarinet playing low tones was accompanied by the swisha-swish-swish of soft percussion. A trumpet picked up a thread, belting a mellow, soulful song through the woods.

The music was nice. I stood for a minute or two, tapping my foot, trying to see through the trees. Then my curiosity got the best of me, and the music pulled me off the path in search of its source. As I picked my way between tree trunks, I thought I saw colors moving back and forth deeper in the woods. As I drew closer, I cast frequent glances over my shoulder, looking for land-marks so I could find my way back. A few yards further, the trees gave way to a scene that stopped me dead in my tracks. I'd never expected to see anything like this in the woods.

I faced a row of colorful vendor stalls lined up wall-to-wall along the edge of a cobblestone plaza. Their fronts were open toward me so I could see the glittering wares inside. Each stall carried something different, and each one seemed more appealing than the one beside it. The sparkle of crystal, the shimmer of gold, and the reflection of sunlight off colorful jewelry drew me closer. There were basket shops with curiously worked weaves in delightful designs, drapery shops that offered rich brocades and shimmering opaque sheers, shoe shops with attractive footwear in desirable styles lined up row upon row. Clothing shops displayed every color in the most exciting fashions ever sewn together, with fabric that flowed, clung, shimmered, floated, and flattered. Soft white wrought iron chairs and tables sat outside a trendy sidewalk café. Wicker seats with comfortably curved arms and posture friendly backs sat at convenient places around the plaza. A beauty salon waited with spritzes, gels, pots, bottles, curlers, combs, and hair dryers to grant any style your heart could desire.

While my eyes took in the tantalizing shops, I also noticed the people. Men and women wandered from store to store, picking things up, examining them, exclaiming about this or that, and often buying. They laughed and teased and hurried to the next shop to see what else they could find. Their apparent joy was contagious, drawing me in, making me want to shop, too.

I moved across the cobblestones and entered a handbag shop. Rummaging through the bags of large and small purses in all different colors was as exciting as a treasure hunt. Some were smooth, some nubby, some had long straps, some were short, and some even came with crossed straps to wear over your back, like a backpack. As I reached for an attractive blue bag, another hand with sparkling rings on the fingers and a jingling bracelet darted around me and grabbed it, yanking it behind me and out of sight.

I whirled around just as a woman said, "This is perfect. I'm buying it." She tossed her long hair, making it shimmer like a blonde waterfall.

"But I was just reaching for it," I said. For some reason, I suddenly felt drawn to the blue bag in the woman's hand so strongly that I wanted it more than any other purse in the shop.

The woman eyed me coolly. "You hadn't touched it yet."

"You saw to that," I said, surprised at the sharpness of my voice.

The woman's brows arched and her eyes traveled down to my feet and back up to my face. "It doesn't suit you," she said. "Besides, you already have," she flicked her hand toward me and quirked up one side of her mouth, "a backpack."

I fumbled with my backpack straps, finally managing to stick my thumbs under them. What was I doing here? Why did I want that blue bag so much? Even though I asked myself the questions, I didn't have answers. Longing for the blue bag stayed stubbornly in my chest. "I was going to trade this for something else," I mumbled.

The woman's voice was too stiff and polite to be nice when she said, "And what could you possibly carry in this while hiking around out there?" She held up the blue bag by its slender strap, jerking her other thumb over her shoulder in the direction of the green woods.

"Just . . . stuff," I said.

"Stuff," the woman repeated, her smile as fake as plastic. "You can put all your stuff in your pack." She handed the shopkeeper some money, then slung the blue bag over her shoulder, swished her hair, and moved to the next stall without looking back.

I handbag shop was no longer fun, so I trudged out toward the plaza.

"Wait," the shopkeeper called, his voice urgent. "You need a new bag." When I turned, he smiled encouragingly. "That pack is outdated." He held up a shiny red bag with a curiously worked clasp. "This would suit you well," he said. "Very stylish, very handy, very beautiful." He leaned closer to me and lowered his voice. "Everyone would want one like it, but there is only one."

The bag swayed a little, catching the light as though winking at me. I was intrigued by the possibility that this purse was even better than the blue one. It wouldn't hurt to take a closer look. I walked slowly toward the shopkeeper, letting my eyes run over the bag's contours, the strap, the clasp. The shopkeeper was right. It certainly was pretty. The clasp was especially suited to my taste. My mind raced over all the possibilities of things I could do with that bag, the people whose heads would turn when they saw me with it over my shoulder. My hands reached for it, but before I even touched it, my pack straps pulled against my shoulders as if holding me back.

Then I blinked, and it seemed as if my vision cleared. Everything was still where it had been before, but it all looked different somehow. The sparkling things seemed tawdry, the shiny leather a pain in the eye, clashing with the simple greens and browns of the uncomplicated woods surrounding them.

I dropped my arms. The bag hung from the shopkeeper's fingers, suddenly garish and ugly, like a red wound. He didn't seem to notice. "Take it," he said, thrusting it toward me. "Hold it."

I shook my head. I knew I didn't need it, and it certainly wouldn't help me get to the estate. My familiar green pack was better suited for what was most important. "No thank you," I said. Then I turned and walked out of the handbag shop and along the row of vendors, my step suddenly light. My hair swished, tickling my neck. I felt curiously free.

"Casey!"

I started at the sound of my name. I turned, surprised and delighted to see shining black hair surrounding Kim's pretty face. She smiled at me above a chiffon gown billowing out in yellow puffs around her slender body. I stared at her, almost unable to believe this was the same girl who wore the baby blue warm up suit this morning.

"Do you like it?" she asked, swaying slightly from side to side.

"It's beautiful," I said, meaning it.

Then I suddenly remembered something. Kim had some explaining to do. I crossed my arms. "How come you got to cross the lake in a boat?"

Kim stopped swaying and looked up at me. "It was just sitting there at the edge of the water," she said. "The captain was on the beach, sunning himself. He said he wasn't using it at the moment, so I could go ahead and take it as long as I got his brother to drive it back after I got to the far shore. So I climbed aboard, rode it across the lake, and found his brother on the other side."

"But the sign said to swim," I reminded her.

Kim shrugged, the yellow chiffon bobbing up and down on her shoulders. "I'm still in the same place I'd be if I swam across, so what difference does it make how I got here?"

I thought about it. What was the difference? Alex seemed to think it mattered, but I couldn't think why. Kim had traveled faster and avoided having rocks thrown at her head. Now we were both in the same shop in the same plaza at the same time, even though I'd struggled to swim my way across the lake. Same place, two different ways.

"Come on, Casey, forget the boat," Kim pleaded. "Please tell me what you really think of my new dress."

I blinked. "It really is pretty," I said, tipping my head. "But it seems kind of . . . puffy."

Casey turned toward a nearby mirror and smoothed her small hands down the full skirt. "I like it," she said. "It makes me feel big."

"Big?"

Casey met my eyes in the mirror. "Yeah. Big enough to matter. Capable of doing things, important things." Her eyes shifted back to her reflection. "It makes me feel brave."

I gave her a dubious look. "It's not a very good walking outfit."

Kim stuck her chin out, an unusual gesture for her. "What's wrong with staying here?"

I took a step back, surprised at her words. "It's not where we wanted to go," I said.

"I don't see what difference it makes," Kim answered. She sidestepped, ducking behind a curtain. I heard the sound of a zipper before she said, "Hand me that shiny blue shirt with the gold beads, will you?"

I looked around and found two piles of clothing hung over the backs of two chairs. The shirt Kim wanted was on top of one pile. I picked it up and tossed it over the curtain. Kim flipped the yellow chiffon back across the curtain to me. "Put that on the 'keep' pile," she said.

"Which one is that?" I asked.

"The one with the green silk pajamas," she said.

I laid the yellow dress over the green silk fabric and tried to pat it into submission, but it kept wanting to slide off. I finally got it to balance well enough that I dared turn away. Kim stood before me in the beaded shirt and navy blue spandex leggings. "I'm getting this, too," she said.

"Kim?" I asked.

"What?"

"All this stuff is more than you need."

Kim planted her fists on her hips. "Since when do you know what I need?"

I put my hands up, palms out. "Don't get mad," I said, realizing this was the first time I'd seen her angry. "I just want you to come to the estate with me."

Kim tugged at her sleeves, adjusting them around her wrists. "I like it here," she said.

"But, why?"

Kim's eyes went wide with disbelief. "Isn't it obvious?" she asked, swinging an arm around at the shops. "All this wonderful stuff!"

I tried to keep my voice calm. "But why do you need it?"

"Because it's pretty." Kim looked around her, then picked up a studded belt. "Because I like it, because everyone else is buying it, and because it makes me feel good," Kim said. "But most of all, I won't be afraid of anyone or anything if I'm dressed like this." She held out her arms. "I'm popular. Can't you see it, Casey? Can't you feel the power of it all?" She bent and picked up a soft, earth-toned dress with the faint imprint of autumn leaves scattered all over the fabric. "Here, try this on."

I glanced at the handbag stall, the bright red bag sitting on top of the other beautiful colors and styles like a cherry on top of a too-sweet confection. I looked at Kim. "No, thanks," I said. "I have what I need."

Kim shook her head. "I don't get you, Casey."

I stared at my friend for a moment. "There's something even better than this up ahead."

Casey looked back at me. "This place is best."

"It's not," I said.

"Is too," Casey replied.

After a moment of strained silence, I asked softly, "So you really won't come with me?"

"No."

"Then, I guess we have to say goodbye," I said, my heart heavy.

Kim looked at me for a moment, then walked forward and wrapped her arms around me.

I hugged her back.

"I hope you find what makes you happy," Kim said. She picked up a cute hat, twirled it in her hands, then popped it on her head. It brought out her dark eyes and made them appear luminous.

I pushed my brown hair back with one hand. "Have you got a headband?" I asked.

Kim's face brightened. "Lots!" she said, bringing out a handful of headbands in all colors I could imagine, some with puffy decorations, some with sparkles, some with animal prints or polka dots.

"May I have one?" I asked.

"Take more than one," she answered, sorting through the pile with eager fingers.

"No, one is enough," I said.

Kim picked out a stretchy blue-green band. "This will compliment your eyes," she said.

"Thank you," I said. I took it and slipped it over my head, pulling the hair back.

"Oh, it's so pretty!" Kim cried. "Are you sure you don't want another one?" she pawed through her mountain of headbands. "Somewhere in here's a silky maroon one with silver threads that would look so good on you."

"No, thanks," I said. "This is enough. Take care, Kim. I love you."

"Love you, too," Kim answered. She gave me a smile, then abandoned the headbands and faced the mirror. She lifted a shining gold chain from the counter and held the necklace up to her throat.

I turned around and walked away through the trees while the clarinet beckoned and the drumbeat tugged at my feet, urging me to stay. I finally reached the path and turned my steps resolutely in the direction I knew I should go.

CHAPTER 8

Even though I wasn't happy about leaving Kim behind, I was glad to be on my way again. Before long, I noticed a scattering of pebbles on the path. They stretched as far as I could see. The small rocks were easy enough to sidestep, but they were annoying. The further I went, the more pebbles I had to avoid. They weren't spread thick enough to make a layer a person could walk on. Instead, they were just close enough that it was hard to find empty places to put my feet. As I picked my way along the path, the pebbles gradually became rocks big enough to twist an uncareful step into a sprained ankle. Annoyance clamped over my heart. If we were supposed to travel this path, then it really ought to be better maintained.

I glanced ahead to see if things got better further along, but it all looked the same. I wondered if I could walk through the trees beside the trail to avoid this irritating pathway. Just as I decided to give it a try, the trail curved. As soon as I turned the bend, I noticed a sign that was the smallest I'd seen yet, but it was plain enough to read. All it said was, "Rake."

Rake?

I slid my fingers through my hair in momentary confusion, then noticed a wooden pole leaning against the signpost. My eyes traveled down it. Sure enough, fastened to the bottom of the pole was a row of hefty metal tines that looked like they meant business. It was a rake. I guessed that I was supposed to rake the path, but everyone except Kim was ahead of me, and she said she wasn't coming, so what good would it do?

Heed the signs.

I drew in a weary breath and let my head fall back, my face pointing up to the ceiling of green leaves above me. They jostled each other as they waited to see what I would do, whispering secrets I couldn't understand.

An unexpected movement of color overhead made me tip my face up to see what it was. A bright yellow balloon rose up through the trees to my right, the string swaying back and forth as the balloon bumped against leaves, nudging them aside to rise higher. It finally burst through the canopy and sailed off through the blue sky, free to go wherever the wind took it.

Where had it come from? Before I could think of anything that could explain it, a faint burst of laughter exploded through the trees. Were there even more shops along here? I didn't really want to find out. I was tired of looking at things I didn't need or have room for.

I reached for the rake, but a sudden burst of applause startled me. What was going on? I left the rake where it was, listening hard at sounds that were quite different from the shops. My curiosity got the better of me, and I walked deeper into the woods. After about fifty yards, I stepped into a clearing that dipped down to accommodate a magnificent sunken amphitheater. I smelled the tantalizing odor of warm popcorn before pinpointing the popcorn cart at the back of the seating area. Beside the crackly paper bags of delicious yellow kernels sat tall glasses of frosty lemonade and shining caramel apples.

Several people sat facing the amphitheater on broad steps that marched down to the front of the stage. The audience's eyes were riveted to the scene before them, their hands dipping in and out of popcorn bags and twirling partially bitten caramel apples while a large man in a fur wrap on stage said, "You let my balloon go because you thought I was a bear?" He turned to stare at the audience with wide, innocent eyes, then said, "I ask you, do bears wear bunny slippers!" He raised a big foot, which, indeed, wore a slipper with a stuffed bunny head and long, furry ears that flopped over the toe.

The audience laughed in delight while the slender woman on

stage wrung her hands. "Oh, Barry," she said, her brow furrowed. "I've been wondering and wondering where those slippers went."

Fascinated, I moved down a couple of stairs and sat down. Soon I was drawn into the story on stage, laughing with the rest of the audience at the antics of the man and woman, along with a portly neighbor who threatened everyone with a water gun and a man dressed as a goat who walked about on hands and knees, looking for any excuse to butt the actors toward the edge of the stage.

When the play ended, I clapped with delight. The performers bowed several times, their smiles wide. Then they made their way to seats in the audience. Before I could decide if it was time for me to leave, several other people stood and moved to the stage. A tall man's gaze swept over the audience and caught my eye. "Hey!" he called, waving his arm in my direction.

"Me?" I asked, casting a glance behind me. There was no one there.

"Yes, you!" he said, a big smile. "We need a brown haired girl for this one. Will you join us, please?"

I shook my head. "I haven't rehearsed," I protested. "I don't know any lines."

"Come on, come on," he said, waving his hand toward the stage. "Your part is easy. You sit on the couch holding a pillow over your stomach, and every time Beatrice, here, says, 'Would you like some soup?' You say, 'I shouldn't have eaten the whole thing.' See? It's easy. You can do it."

The honey-haired Beatrice bounded toward me, her hand held out in invitation. She was in front of me before I could turn and run. "It's fun," she said, her amber eyes sparkling. "I'll help you."

It seemed there was nothing I could do but let her lead me onstage. As instructed, I curled up in one corner of a couch, my arms wrapped around a couch pillow to hold it to my stomach. I was sure the audience could see it bumping up and down from the pounding of my frightened heart. Then the play began.

I was so nervous I didn't even pay attention to the other actor's lines. The first time Beatrice trotted over to the couch, leaned over, and asked in a high falsetto voice, "Would you like some soup?" I had to swallow twice before I could answer in a shaky voice, "I shouldn't have eaten the whole thing." The audience burst into laughter. I gazed at them in surprise. That wasn't even my best effort, and they were clapping for me. My heart warmed, and my stomach went from feeling sick to tickling with anticipation.

I had three more chances to recite my line. Each time, I said it better than the first, and the audience laughed and clapped. When the play was over, I hopped off the couch and lined up to bow with the rest of the cast, the pillow still clutched to my stomach, which made the audience laugh again. The happy sound of their voices surrounded me, lifting my spirits. This was fun. I didn't want to leave the stage, but Beatrice took hold of my arm and led me down into the audience.

I seated myself closer to the stage with my own bag of popcorn and a cold drink to watch another play, then another, each one better than the last. I relaxed against my backpack, perfectly comfortable.

In the back of my mind was the vague memory that I was on a journey and it was time to leave now, but I was having too much fun. There was no big hurry. I was happy and the path would still be there later. After all, this wasn't a race.

I leaned over to Beatrice and whispered, "May I perform again?"

She smiled at me. "Oh, yes. You may have as many turns as you like. Just stick around."

I sat back, utterly content to wonder what part I would play next. Would it be funny? Or tragic? I could be like the goat man, providing comic relief, or I could be the heroic star. My cheeks hurt from smiling. I shifted my pack to support my head better, and that's when I realized I'd had enough to drink that I needed a bathroom. When I whispered to Beatrice, she pointed toward a little building at the back of the seating area next to the concession stand. I slid my arms into my pack straps and hurried up the steps to the rest rooms. I was in such a hurry that I pushed on one of the doors before I noticed the male silhouette fastened to it. I veered off to the next door, which greeted me with a female silhouette. I hurried inside, but my mind was no longer filled with possible roles for my next play. I couldn't get the image of the restroom silhouettes out of my mind. The male had a beard and hiking boots, the female had hair styled like mine and wore a headband.

CHAPTER 9

I came out of the restroom and glanced down the amphitheater steps toward Beatrice. I wanted to wave goodbye, but her eyes were riveted to the stage. With a sinking heart, I realized that she'd probably never notice I was gone.

I turned away and trudged toward the path, but to my surprise, every step I took became lighter. What caused this increased happiness? Was it possible that the theater was evil? By putting distance between me and the stage, was I loosening some terrible power it held over me?

But that didn't make sense. Once I'd gotten used to it, performing brought me joy. Laughter was not a bad thing. The experience had given me greater confidence, plus provided refreshment, rest, and a bathroom. But what if I'd stayed longer? That would have created a problem. The theater wasn't my final destination, so it was time for me to move on. But as I walked, I couldn't help harboring the hope that there would be a theater on the estate.

I reached the sign that said, "Rake," adjusted the straps of my pack, and rolled my neck, taking in a deep breath. I had more energy now that before. The breath rushed out of my lungs as I faced the sign.

"Rake."

I pushed my sleeves up and grabbed the rake handle, raking the path with broad sweeps, pulling the rocks off to one side. Lucky for me the path wasn't very wide. After moving a few yards down the trail, my arms were tired and my back was getting sore. A sudden thought struck me. If Alex had gone ahead, then why wasn't the path already cleared? He seemed so determined to follow the signs, even to the point of finding fault with Kim's boat ride. Could he have missed the sign? He was rather tall, and the sign was small. What about Megan? She must have gone this way, too. They couldn't both have missed the sign, could they? Was it possible they'd gone another way? I didn't see how. Maybe they'd just decided not to rake. And if no one else raked, then why should I?

I nearly laid the rake down so I could continue on without it, but my heart wouldn't let me. My shoulders sagged. It didn't matter what anyone else did. It mattered what I did. And right now, it was just me, the sign, and the rake.

I continued slowly, raking as I went, and soon found my rhythm. Rake, step, rake, step. I didn't feel the deep ache in my shoulders until I stopped at the next curve in the road where the trees suddenly ended. They abandoned the rocky path to make its own way through a meadow. But instead of lush grass tangling in the wind, this field was choked with bruise-purple blossoms made of clusters of short spikes crowding up to the edge of the trail. The dark green stems beneath the dangerous flowers were waist high, bristling with spines and raggedy sharp-edge leaves.

Stretching my sore back muscles, I wiped sweat off my face and looked down the path, trying to gauge my risk of being skewered by thistles. I was again tempted to stop raking right then and there, to just drop the tool and go on the best I could.

Heed the signs.

The memory of intense eyes locked on mine made the ghost of a shiver shake my whole body. I tore my eyes away from the thistles and poured the energy of frustration into my lonely task. Rake, step, rake, step. To my great relief, the number of rocks diminished as I made my way through the thistles. By the time I finally reached the end of the meadow and stepped into the cooling shade of trees on the other side, the path ahead of me was as clear as the one I'd left behind.

I felt surprisingly good. Not only had I cleared the way for myself, but now anyone who happened to follow would have smooth going. I pulled myself up tall, allowing my cramped back muscles a luxurious stretch. I glanced behind me, ready to revel in a job well done.

A few yards past the forest I'd left behind, a blonde head bobbed up and down in the corridor between the thistles. I knew that hair. It was stuck on the head of the blonde kid from the cliff. Rock Boy. He was busy doing something on the path, something involving a long handle that made his shoulders move from side to side.

"Hey!" I called. "What are you doing?"

The boy looked up. In spite of the distance between us, I couldn't miss the wicked grin that spread across his face. He raised a broom over his head. "This path is so smooth and boring," he called back. "But there are all these rocks along one side. So I'm spreading them out to make the way more interesting."

"You stop that!" I hollered.

He bent back over his broom and swept again. Imagining another pile of rocks scattering over the trail, my anger blazed. "Stop right now!" I yelled. "I just cleared that path! Don't you dare mess it up!"

The boy looked up again, stuck his tongue out at me, and went back to undoing everything I'd just accomplished.

It was maddening.

I took a few steps back along the trail, thinking that I'd meet up with the scoundrel and take his broom away. The boy must have read my mind. He looked up, saw me, and danced back toward the far line of trees, the broom held up over his head. He could easily be long gone by the time I reached the spot where he sashayed with the broom, taunting me.

It wasn't worth the chase. I'd only lose time. It was hard to think of him undoing all the work I'd done, but trying to catch him now would only put me further behind. Let the little bounder do as he liked, I was going on.

I turned away and strode among the trees without another backward glance. I tried not to think about what Rock Boy was doing, but it already had its effect on me. Instead of soaring on the wings of satisfaction at a job well done, I staggered down the trail under a heavy burden of disappointment and sore muscles.

CHAPTER 10

I calculated that it was around mid-day. My stomach argued with me, insisting that we'd been traveling this winding path for days and days, but it was prone to exaggerate when it was hungry.

The trees along the trail had thinned again, separating enough to reveal a pleasant spot with a large, smooth rock just a little way off the path. A patch of soft grass surrounded it, and a stream played tag with floating leaves as it bubbled past. I was more than ready to eat the lunch that our host said was in our packs.

After checking the ground for stickers and finding not so much as a stone, I settled myself on the cushiony grass and unzipped my pack. I pulled out a double palm-sized package that was cool to the touch. Inside was an ice-cold drink in a foil pouch, nestled next to a waxed paper package that proved to be a sandwich, cut in half. There was an apple, a container of crispy, salted potato sticks, and two cookies that were fat and puffy with oatmeal and smelled like cinnamon. I was so hungry that I worried this might not be enough food for me, but it was certainly better than nothing.

After giving thanks, I sank my teeth into one of the sandwich halves. Before I even had a chance to swallow, something sailed through the air and thudded onto the grass beside me. Startled, I looked down. I couldn't believe my eyes. I parted the blades of grass as I chewed, my jaws grinding together faster and faster when I saw that my first suspicion was correct.

Someone had thrown a rock at me.

I whirled around. Sure enough, Rock Boy with the saucy gray

eyes stood on the trail, hefting a rock in his palm as he studied my reaction.

"You little twerp, you could have hit me with that thing!" I shouted, barely remembering to set my sandwich aside as I jumped to my feet.

The kid took a step back. "Yeah, well, I didn't," he said. His gaze shifted from me to the food on the ground beside me. "Whatcha got there?"

"It's my lunch," I snapped. "And if you'd quit throwing rocks, I could eat it in peace."

"What is it?" the boy asked, his eyes opening wider as he tried to identify each shape.

"Sorry, no rock sandwiches, so you wouldn't be interested," I snarled.

The boy drew back as if I'd slapped him. He blinked a few times, but it wasn't enough to stop his eyes from welling up with tears. Doubt crowded my mind, followed by a twinge of regret for speaking so harshly. Did this kid with rocks on his brain really have feelings? In the silence that followed, I heard a faint rumble. I instinctively put my hand to my stomach, but it wasn't me whose stomach was growling.

The kid rubbed a fist across his eyes and tried on a sneer. "Aw, I'll bet you've just got rotten apples and moldy old bread," he said too loudly. He crossed his arms over his middle and squeezed them in tightly, just as I would have done if I'd been trying to pacify an empty stomach when I had no food.

I considered the situation. I was pretty hungry. I knew I could eat every scrap of food I had, and probably want more. I had a journey ahead of me. Who knew how long this unexpected detour would take? This kid was a pain. He'd tried to bean me with rocks while I was swimming in the lake, and he'd made a mess of all the work I'd done to clear the path. I had sore muscles but no satisfaction.

And he was hungry.

There were no signs here to tell me what to do. But I didn't need a sign. I knew.

I sighed. "Well, then, you can have the rotten apple and I'll take the moldy bread." The boy darted suspicious eyes to my face, searching for the truth behind my words. I pointed to his hand, the one that still clutched a rock. "You'll have to drop that first, though," I said. "There are no rocks on the menu today."

He still stared at me.

I sat back down on the grass and folded the untouched sandwich half back in the waxed paper. I held it out toward the boy. With my other hand, I picked up the bitten half of sandwich and took another bite. "One for me," I said through the food in my mouth, "and one for you." I lifted the wrapped sandwich in invitation.

The boy dropped the rock and moved closer. Finally, he reached out and took the sandwich, then stepped back to unwrap it. He was hungry, no doubt about it. He finished his sandwich half before I did. I tossed him the juice packet, and he downed that in two gulps. I was glad I had a water bottle for myself. We shared the cookies and the potato sticks, but somehow he ended up with the apple. Yet after he'd mowed down more than half of it with his teeth, he suddenly stopped. I wondered if he'd bitten his tongue. He looked at the apple, chewing thoughtfully, then looked at me. He pushed his mouthful of fruit into a bulge in one cheek. Then he extended the apple in my direction. "Want some?" I looked into his gray eyes, wide and hopeful.

"Sure," I said, taking the apple from him. "Thanks." And I took a bite.

CHAPTER 11

Rock Boy took off along the trail back the way he'd come.
I thought I heard him call, "Thanks" as he disappeared around
the first bend, but I wasn't sure. I started down the trail in the
opposite direction. My pack rode light on my back, whether
because the lunch was gone or because I had extra energy from
the food, I wasn't sure. But I was full. Really full. I shouldn't be
this satisfied after eating only half a lunch, but I was.

Then it occurred to me that I had done nothing to earn the
food I'd just eaten. I deserved it no more than the boy I'd shared
it with. I wondered if his stomach was as content as mine.

I strode along the trail, feeling good. Things were turning out
all right.

Thunk . . . thunk . . . thunk.

I stopped, startled at the sound of metal on metal in this
wooded place.

Thunk . . . thunk . . .thunk.

The ominous sound didn't belong here, so I hurried my steps,
not wanting to know what was behind it. Suddenly it stopped,
and I heard a familiar sigh. I stopped dead in my tracks. Could it
really be him? And if it was, what was he doing here? "Alex?" I
called in a cautious voice.

After a moment of tense silence, Alex's voice called back,
"Hello? Casey? Is that you?"

"Yes, it's me!" Caution transformed to joy at the sound of his
voice. "Where are you?"

"Over here."

"Are you all right?"

"Sure! I've never been better."

Still a little wary, I asked, "What was that noise?"

His delighted laugh tickled my heart. "I'm just lifting weights. Come on over."

When I found him, Alex stood in front of a three-walled plaza with a sloping roof. The back wall stretched long enough to shelter an array of exercise equipment that included everything anyone would need for bodybuilding. Alex's bare arms bulged with muscle when he lifted a corner of the towel draped around his neck and wiped his sweating brow. Then he moved in and gave me a hug.

"Wow, you look great," I said against his shirt.

"Thanks," he said, stepping back to give me a heart-stopping grin. "Working out is amazing. Come try it." He waved an arm toward a weight bench behind him. There were several metal rings of descending size on either side of a bar suspended above the bench.

"I can't lift that," I said.

Alex easily pulled off the weights until there was a single small disc on either side. "There," he said. "Come on. I'll help you." I lay down on the bench and took the cold bar in my hands. "Ready?" Alex asked. "Now, lift!"

I pressed upward, the bar heavy against my palms. As soon as I straightened my arms, Alex said, "Lower it." I bent my elbows and brought the weight down. "Up again," Alex said, his white teeth grinning in delight. I pressed the bar up, feeling the pressure in my arms and shoulders. It felt kind of good. "Lower it," Alex said.

I did.

"Can you do another one?" Alex asked, his eyes anxious. I didn't answer because I didn't want to break my concentration. I pushed up again, straightening my arms, sending that metal bar to the limit of my reach. I felt strong and powerful. I was happy. This time when I brought the bar down, I let it land in the metal brackets. Thunk . . . thunk. I sat up, my face flushed, muscles tingling.

"Do you want to try something else?" Alex asked.

I nodded. I soon discovered that some things were easier to work than others. Riding the stationary bike felt like flying. The ski track was awkward, making my limbs flail about like spaghetti. After I worked up a good sweat, I sat on a webbed chair while Alex got me a cold fruit drink. I took a sip. It was icy and delicious. Dabbing my head with Alex's extra towel, I asked, "How'd you find this place?"

"By accident," Alex said, settling into the chair next to mine. "Traveling that path got pretty boring, so I decided to make it more challenging."

"Hey," I said. "Those rocks all over the path by the thistle meadow were a pretty good challenge."

Alex's brow creased. "You found rocks on the path?" he asked. "But I raked them off."

"They didn't stay that way," I said, and filled my mouth with cold fruit juice.

"I can't figure it out," Alex said.

I swallowed and said, "I think we all had to rake the path, but that's behind us now. You were saying you wanted more of a challenge?"

Alex cleared his throat. "Well, I decided to walk through the trees beside the path, looking for uneven ground in order to work different leg muscles. At one point I glanced over and spotted this set-up here. I was pretty surprised, let me tell you, but it was a lucky find."

I looked around at the shiny exercise equipment. "It's strange that no one else comes here," I said.

"They do," Alex answered. "There are living quarters on the other side of the exercise plaza." He jerked his thumb toward the wall.

A cold premonition washed over me. "But . . . you're not staying," I said.

"Why not?" Alex asked. "I love the way a good workout makes me feel, and this is better than any walk through the woods."

I set the juice glass down on a nearby table. "We're on a journey, remember?" I asked, trying to keep voice calm.

"I was on a journey," Alex said. "I found my destination."

I pushed myself to my feet. "This is not where we were headed," I said, my stomach tying in knots.

"Listen, Casey, it was kind of fun at first. We hiked, we swam, but then it was just walking and walking through the woods. I'm tired of doing the same thing over and over."

"Please, Alex." Panic rose in my voice, making it come out tight and squeaky. Mind racing, I searched for the right words, ones that would convince him to come with me. "Let's go." I held out my hand for him to take.

Alex gazed at my face, then scanned the row of gleaming machines. He turned back to me. "Sorry, Casey, I like it here. I want you to stay with me."

My fingers laced and unlaced themselves. "Don't you remember our host?" I asked. Alex's brow darkened, but .I pressed on. "What did he say before you started?"

Alex put his hands out, palms up. "I have followed the signs, and where did they get me? Just to more signs. I'm tired of signs, Casey. I'm happy here. What's wrong with that?"

"You could do better," I said, grabbing my pack straps to still my worrying fingers.

Alex folded his muscled arms. "It's good to exercise."

"It is," I said, my mind scrambling for ways to help Alex see where his choices were leading him. "But spending all your time exercising is a very narrow way to live."

"That's because you haven't done enough, Casey," Alex said, taking my elbow and tugging me toward a hinged machine with pads. "Try this one again, you liked it, I could tell."

I pulled away. "I did like it," I admitted, "but I don't love it. It was fun, and I'd like to do it again some time, but right now I have more important things to do. You have more important things to do, too."

"But I don't want to do anything else," Alex said. "I'm not doing anything wrong."

I looked up at Alex's handsome face to see it set hard with determination. It was true, he wasn't doing anything wrong. But he wasn't doing what was best. My heart jumped as I reached up to brush his dark, curly hair with my fingers. "I'm scared, Alex."

"Why?"

"I don't want to go on alone."

"Then stay with me," he said, his face relaxing into an inviting smile.

I shook my head and swallowed the lump in my throat. "No. I need to go."

"I need to stay here."

My heart fell like a cold lump of ice. "Well," I sighed, stepping away from Alex. With no hope, I said, "Maybe I'll see you later."

"Maybe you'll come back," Alex answered.

"Good bye," I said, my eyes filling with tears.

"Bye," he answered. As I walked back toward the path, I heard his soft voice say, "Love you, Casey."

Chapter 12

As the afternoon aged, the sides of the path rose higher and higher until they were higher than the top of my head and funneled me into a twelve-foot-wide canyon. Without sunlight, I walked hunched and chilled in the canyon's shadow. The walls weren't straight, so I couldn't see very far ahead. Unsure what direction I was headed, I shifted from side to side as the walls angled one way and then another. Claustrophobia made me glance up repeatedly to make sure there was still sky overhead. Would this canyon never end?

I brought my gaze down from another check of the sky and saw someone standing further along the canyon. My heart leaped with hope. Now I wouldn't have to travel this desolate place alone. "Hello?" I called.

The person turned his face toward me and his arm went up in greeting. "Casey!" called a familiar voice from a long time ago.

"Derrick!" I yelled. I broke into a run, and his arms opened. I ran into them and hugged him tight. He laughed and picked me up off my feet. I laughed, too. As soon as he set me down, I stepped back and asked, "What are you doing here?"

"Looking for a friend," he said.

"You found one," I cried, my heart light with joy. "Let's walk together." I took a step down the canyon, grabbing Derrick's hand to pull him along with me. To my surprise, Derrick pulled his hand free. I looked back at him, puzzled. "What's wrong?"

"Why are you going that way?" Derrick asked patiently.

"It's the way we're supposed to go." I answered. "Where have you been since this morning?"

Derrick grinned. "If you really want to know, I walked through a beautiful green valley full of flowers, filled with the music of a running stream. There were dozens of kinds of fruit trees, all ripe, and everything I ate was delicious. Bright birds flew everywhere, there were tame animals of all sorts, along with comfortable benches where I could rest whenever I felt like it."

I stared at him, hardly believing. "Derrick, are you feeling all right?"

"Just great," he said with a freckled grin. "Even better since I saw you."

I glanced down the barren canyon, then chose my words carefully. "Derrick, does this look like a valley of green trees to you? Do you hear any birds, or see any water?" I leaned closer, not wanting to miss his answer.

Derrick's eyes went wide, and he studied me intently. "Casey, are you all right?"

"Yes," I said, my voice steady. "Just answer, please."

Derrick took hold of my shoulders. "What I see here is a barren canyon, a place where no living thing should be. The place I'm talking about is through there." He let go of my shoulder with one hand and pointed to a wide fissure in the rock behind him. It was narrower than the canyon, only one person wide.

I stared at it for a moment at the rough edged rock, as barren as the rest of the canyon. I said hesitantly, "You came through there?"

"Yeah." Derrick used the hand that remained on my shoulder to turn me toward the fissure. "Right through there, just a few dozen yards, is paradise, my dear Casey. Let's go. I'll carry your pack." He propelled me forward into the fissure while tugging on my backpack.

"Just a minute," I said, planting my feet and letting my legs go stiff.

Derrick quit pushing. "What's wrong?"

"I don't know what's in there," I said.

Derrick laughed. "I just told you."

"But I don't really know."

"It's there, trust me. Have I ever lied to you?"

A gust of fresh air blew against my face, scented with lush grass, greenery, flowers, and the unmistakable coolness of water. I inhaled and closed my eyes.

"See?" Derrick said, his voice light.

I opened my eyes and managed to turn in the narrow fissure to face Derrick. "Have you been to the estate?" I asked.

Derrick spread his hands. "Not to the house proper, but I suspect those are the grounds through there. I tell you, Casey, I've traveled through some wonderful landscapes. It's all so marvelous, you've got to see for yourself. I expect to come across the mansion any time now."

"But, Derrick, the signs said to go this way." I gestured toward the barren canyon.

Derrick grinned, then pointed to a scrawny post that appeared to lean from the weight of a small sign fastened on top. The sign read, "This way," with an arrow pointing toward the fissure. My eyes widened in surprise.

"So," Derrick said, his voice eager. "You don't have to go that way." He pointed down the canyon. "Why would anyone want to go there anyway?" He shuddered. "Come on, let's go. We'll both follow the sign."

"Just a minute," I said, reaching out to give the sign a pat. It wobbled. I took hold of the sign and twisted. It turned easily in my hand, pivoting on a post sitting loosely in the ground.

"Derrick?" I asked, my eyes on the sign.

"Who cares?" Derrick said, his voice urgent. "When you see where I've been, you won't want to be anywhere else. Forget those signs, they're all confusing anyway, and who knows who put what sign where? Anyone could put a sign up and make it point in any direction."

My voice came out quiet. "Like you did?"

Derrick was silent for a moment, then he laughed, but it sounded harsh. "Yeah, like I did. See how easy it is to put up your own sign? Come on, Casey, we'll find the estate together."

I glanced behind me through the fissure, where I couldn't see but could sense the greenness and comfort of a place beyond. It was sorely tempting to go see Derrick's paradise. What if I went for a while? If we didn't happen to find the estate, I would come back to the canyon. If Derrick had found the way through the fissure to this place, surely I could, too.

"Where did you get the sign, Derrick?" I asked.

He snorted. "Sign, sign, sign, can't you think of anything else?"

"Where did you get it?"

He jabbed his finger across the canyon. "Over there. Big deal."

I glanced across the path and saw a hole in the dirt against the opposite wall. If the sign were stuck in that hole with the lettering visible, the arrow would point down the canyon the same way I was traveling.

Heed the signs.

As tempting as it was to walk in soft grass and pick fruit straight from the trees, I knew it was only a temporary diversion. And if I got too comfortable, I may not want to come back. "Derrick," I said, "I don't believe the estate is through there." I indicated the fissure with my thumb.

Derrick's face fell. "Casey, I'm lonely."

I grabbed his hands in mine. "Then come with me," I said. I pushed past him, into the canyon, turning him around as I walked.

Derrick's brows lowered. "I don't want to go that way."

"We'll follow the signs together," I urged. "Come on, Derrick, we can make it. I'll help you."

Derrick's jaw shot out in a stubborn pout. "It's too hard," he said. He pulled his hands free of mine and folded his arms across his chest, leaning back toward the rock and bumping the loose sign. It fell over. Derrick didn't seem to notice. "Come with me, Casey. Please."

I stared at my friend's immovable face. I'd never seen him without a smile before. He looked different, like a stranger. Derrick's features blurred as my eyes filled with tears. "Oh, Derrick, what can I say to make you come with me?" I begged.

"I could ask the same of you," Derrick said, his voice hard.

There was a lump in my throat so big I could hardly speak. I had to swallow a couple of times before I could get out a single word. "Nothing."

"Me neither," he said, and turned his face away.

"Derrick," I said, moving close enough to hug him. I couldn't get my arms all the way around because he still leaned against the rock, but I squeezed him the best I could. When I pulled away, I looked up at his face to see a tear glinting in his eye. He dashed it away with a clenched fist, then turned and entered the fissure. In a few steps, he was gone. I stared at the opening for a few moments, hoping against hope that he might change his mind and come back. But the crack in the rock was empty.

With a heavy heart, I bent and picked up the sign. I carried it over to the hole it came from and pushed it into the earth. It stood straight, pointing the way down the canyon. "This way." I gave it a pat, turned away from the fissure and moved on slow feet down the canyon.

CHAPTER 13

Soon after leaving Derrick, the canyon wall to the right of me flattened out while the left wall rose even higher, forming a real, honest-to-goodness mountain. It was not a scenic mountain like you'd find on a picture postcard, with a bubbling stream laughing over polished stones, or stately pine trees climbing up its sides to cast deep green shade over soft patches of moss. This mountain was a huge mound of dirt scarred by erosion. Jagged wounds opened around sharp chunks of partially buried rock, gray as dirty ice. The place was so barren, it was repulsive. I shivered and hurried along, anxious to put it behind me.

Suddenly, the path I trod took a sharp upward turn, winding its way up the side of the barren mountain. A sign beside the crooked path read, "Climb." My head drooped and I dropped to the ground. It was the hottest part of the afternoon, and my heart still hurt from encounters with Derrick, Alex, and Kim. What I wanted most of all was to lie in cool shade and rest. If I absolutely had to move, couldn't I at least walk under a canopy of leaves? I wondered for the hundredth time what Derrick was doing right now. I missed him, but I had made the right decision. I was almost sure of it.

So, you decided to go this way, so you'd better get going. I took a swig from my water bottle. The warm water was not refreshing, but at least it was wet. I pressed my hands to the rough, dry ground and pushed myself up onto my feet. After a couple of steps, the path inclined beneath my sneakers. Step, step, step. I moved automatically, without thinking, going a good two-dozen weary steps up the path before a flash of bright red off to the side made me turn my head. I could scarcely believe the shiny tram sitting at a station several dozen yards away. The attached cable swayed just a little, beckoning to me.

Pure relief shot through me as I eagerly retraced my steps to flat ground and headed for the tram. My legs found new strength in the promise of a ride over this forbidding mountain.

On the opposite side of the station, I discovered a group of thirty people clustered together, all facing the same direction. I crowded in behind tehm, curious to see what held their attention. When I saw Megan standing in front of the assembly, I broke into a smile. Her loose hair hung full about her face, her eyes shining as she leaned forward and said, "You may all come. Everyone is welcome."

When murmurs arose from the crowd, I took advantage of the disturbance to call out, "Megan!"

Megan looked in my direction, sifting through the faces until she found mine. "Casey!" she cried, her green eyes widening, her arm waving in my direction. With a jolt of alarm, I saw that her wrist was bandaged, the white fabric stark white against her skin. She darted a glance around the waiting crowd, making eye contact here and there. "Excuse me," she said to no one in particular. "I'll be right back."

Megan hurried forward and grabbed me in a brief embrace, hard enough to make me wince. When she pulled back, I asked, "What happened to your wrist?"

"Oh," Megan lifted her hand and inspected the bandage as though seeing it for the first time. "I tripped on some rocks while raking and got a sprain."

"You raked, too?"

Megan gave me a curious look. "Sure I raked, so there was nothing for you to do."

"There were rocks on the path," I said.

"But that doesn't make sense," Megan replied, puzzled.

"It had to do with a boy who likes to throw rocks," I said.

"Oh," she said, rolling her eyes. "Him."

"Never mind about that now," I said. "Does it hurt?"

"Not any more." Megan lowered her arm and rested her hand on my shoulder. "Just look at them, Casey." Megan's face was alight. "They all want to join our journey."

I took in the crowd with a dubious gaze. I no longer felt comfortable about riding the tram. With Megan's leadership, I knew I could follow the signs, which was the right thing to do. It wouldn't be as hard as taking that barren path on my own. "I hope they all have their own water bottles."

Megan flipped her head and her hair shivered down her back. "We don't need to worry about that. We're taking the tram."

My heart nearly stopped. Even though I'd walked over to the station planning to ride the tram, I knew in my heart it wasn't right. The sign said, "Climb." "But that's against the rules," I protested.

"Think about it," Megan said patiently. "How would we get all these people over the mountain before dark if we climbed? The ends justify the means, Casey. I'm doing the greater good by getting these people to the estate quickly."

Her words plucked a strange chord in my heart, but I didn't bother sorting it out. If Megan rode the tram, then I would, too, and simply be glad for a friend and traveling companion. "I'm with you," I said.

Megan stared at me a moment, then her mouth quirked in an apologetic smile. "I'm sorry, Casey, there isn't room for you." Dumbstruck, I gazed at the tram, the people, then to the tram again. I couldn't deny that it looked like a tight fit. I swallowed my disappointment and asked, "Who else is staying behind?"

Megan's eyes dropped to her wrist bandage, which suddenly needed adjusting. "You've got to understand, Casey, I didn't know you were coming. We had just enough riders before you got here."

Heat bloomed in my cheeks. "You mean I'm the only one staying behind?"

Megan glanced up and nodded. "For now. But don't worry, you can ride the tram after it comes back."

I stared at the stranger before me, the one who looked like Megan, but didn't talk like her. My voice was louder than I meant it to be when I said, "You're not following the signs."

Megan blinked, her expression calm. "These are unusual

circumstances."

"I'll say they are," I said, my voice rising. "I thought I'd found a friend, but all I got was a traitor."

"Casey, you're not being fair," Megan said, folding her arms. "These people were here before you."

"And we were on this journey together," I said, unmoved by her words. "I'm not waiting for your stupid tram to come back," I snapped. "I'm following the signs."

"Come on, Casey, don't be like that," Megan said, putting her hand on my shoulder. The tram bell sounded. People funneled into the shiny red car. I turned and walked away.

"Just wait here," Megan said. "It won't be long. I'll meet you on the other side."

I didn't stop, didn't answer, didn't look back. Masking hurt with anger, I marched to the signpost and whacked it with my hand. It didn't budge. I made a hard turn on the ball of my foot to face the mountain. I strode upward, my calves not yet begging for mercy when the tram rumbled past me toward the top of the mountain. In spite of myself, I stared at it as it shambled up and up and up.

A familiar face appeared in one of the crowded tram windows, surrounded by a cloud of red hair. Megan raised her bandaged arm and waved. Her smile ignited my deepest envy. Out of habit, I managed to lift my hand in her direction, but I couldn't summon enough energy to wave, and there was no trace of a smile on my face.

Heed the signs.

But I didn't want to! I was tired. Riding the tram would be much easier. After all, I'd been scratched, whipped, nearly drowned by a rock-throwing brat, endured sore muscles from raking in vain, and even shared my lunch without a sign telling me to. I hadn't stayed to shop with Kim, or let the theater people draw me in, at least not for long, and I'd left Alex behind. I had even resisted Derrick's plea to follow him to paradise. Didn't that give me extra points?

I dropped my head and rubbed my palm against my forehead, trying to talk myself into taking the easy way. Then I turned around and read the sign at the bottom of the mountain again with dull eyes.

"Climb."

I turned toward the mountain and lifted my palm to my forehead, making a visor over my eyes. I watched the tram top the mountain, its window shooting back gleams of reflected light from the lowering sun. I stared at it until it slid over the summit and disappeared from view.

My head pounded, then subsided to a quiet burble, like clear water. Weighing my feelings, it dawned on me that trams eventually rust away, while water is constant. The words of our host again flowed through my memory, like water. Heed the signs.

"Climb."

I took a hesitant step upward. Then another. And another. My steps came swifter as my heart tugged me onward, rushing me up the path as though someone much stronger was giving me a boost. It took no effort on my part to get halfway up the mountainside, but once the slope beneath me was longer than the one above, the marvelous burst of energy left and I struggled onward.

The climb was more difficult than it had seemed from ground level. Sometimes the path disappeared altogether and I had to guess the way over and around rocks and boulders. I stubbed my toes, stumbled and fell, tore my pants, scraped my legs and the palms of my hands. I stepped on a rock the wrong way and turned my foot. It wasn't a bad sprain, but made me step lightly to keep pressure off my injured ankle. The climb was harder than anything else I'd done, harder than pushing through bramble bushes, swimming the lake, or raking rocks. So intent was I on watching my footing that I didn't realize I'd reached the summit until the path fell away. I stared dumbly at a descending mountainside that was at least as rocky as the one I'd just climbed.

I sank to the ground, elbows on knees, dropping my head onto crossed arms. When my breathing was regular, I wearily lifted my head, then froze. The incredible beauty of deep orange clouds filtering bright beams of golden sunlight nearly took my breath away. The view from here was worth every hardship and disappointment. I was grateful to be right where I was at this very moment. My skin tingled, and a rush of warmth flowed from my head through my body and out of my toes. I wanted to stay and watch until the sun burned itself out, but I knew it would be wiser to get off the mountain before darkness fell. I took a final look at the magical sky, memorizing the glory of it before starting down the narrow trail. I don't know if gravity was the reason, but descending turned out to be much easier than the climb. The sun wasn't even touching the horizon when I reached flat ground.

I needed to hurry.

CHAPTER 14

The trail led through a forbidding landscape stained ocher. The rocky mountain behind me surrendered to hills of barren sand undulating across my field of vision like a prehistoric monster. My spirit sagged. I was hungry again, and I'd drunk all my water. I didn't feel like walking through sand dunes. I hated grit in my sneakers. Where was the estate, anyway? Who was keeping score? When would I get a break?

My eyes caught sight of a dun-colored sign that was all but invisible in front of a background of sand. The sign read, "This way," along with a black arrow pointing straight across the barren expanse.

I didn't want to go, but realized I wouldn't arrive at all by standing here feeling sorry for myself. I started walking as fast as I could across the shifting surface. I'd only gone a few yards when my shoes filled with sand, making my feet slither on the insole. Frustrated, I stopped to pull off my shoes and socks. Holding my shoes by their laces, I trudged off through the dunes, warm sand hugging my toes. The going was much easier barefoot.

It was hard to tell how far I'd gone because one pile of sand looked pretty much like another, except for one huge ten-story tall dune directly in my path. If I had to climb over that, I didn't see how I could possibly make it to the estate before dark. Going around would take just as long. It made me tired just to look at, so I lowered my head and trudged on.

In spite of the clouds and the lowering sun, I was hot. I

wished I could rest, but I was desperate to reach the estate before being blinded by night. An unexpected breeze snuck up behind me and cooled the sweat on my arms. A moment later, I welcomed another curious swirl of wind stirring my hair and cooling my scalp. I took a deep breath, thanking my lucky stars for this small but fortunate blessing. A moment later, a stronger gust of air pushed me forward, stinging my skin with sharp grains of sand. I turned toward the traitor wind, my eyes narrowed in self-defense. Then they widened in astonishment at the sight of increasing wind whipping the sand into a funnel that reached up into the sky, a tenuous thread stitching it to the clouds. It undulated in slow, snaky movements, as if watching me to see what I would do.

I ran.

Tiny missiles of sand pursued, stinging my exposed skin without mercy. Hair whipped my eyes, trying to separate from my head. There was so much sand in the air that it was hard to find oxygen. It swirled so viciously that I wondered how long it would take to flay me alive. In my headlong flight through the dizzying cloud, I tripped over something that screamed. I fell, dazed and confused for a moment, trying to breathe, wondering if maybe I had screamed. Then I felt something grab my ankle, and the next scream was definitely mine.

"Help . . . me . . ." someone said in a voice breathless with fear.

"Kim?" I asked, and got sand in my mouth.

"Casey!" Kim cried. "Help!"

I didn't bother asking what she was doing here. I reached out toward her and my hand hit something hard and rough. I stretched further. My fingers curled over the top of the hard thing and felt space. Could it be a cave? I crawled forward, dragging Kim, and stuck my head over the edge of rock. I was rewarded with instant relief from the sand battering my face. The cave was beneath the rock overhang. "Kim!" I cried. "This way!"

A wail pierced through the screaming wind. "I can't!"

I scooted back from the shelter and my skin shrank in protest. I hurriedly felt my way down to Kim's hand around my ankle. The sooner I got her to move, the sooner I would be sheltered, too. I grabbed her hand and pulled hard. "Come on!" I yelled. Sand coated my tongue and crunched between my teeth when I gritted them together. Kim came, crawling and whimpering. I scrambled over the lip of rock, pulling Kim with me. We fell over the edge, tumbling only about four feet until we hit sand firm enough to stop our fall. I shoved Kim underneath the rock. She moaned and curled up inside the shelter. I pushed myself in after her. The shelter was only about three feet high, enough to scrunch under, but not enough to sit up. "Move in," I cried, feeling the sand pelt my shoulders on either side of my backpack.

"I can't," Kim moaned.

I squished up against the pack on her back and reached past her. My fingers bumped against a rock wall. It was true. She really couldn't move in any further, which meant that I couldn't, either. I pressed in as close as I could, grateful for my backpack. I spat to clear my mouth while Kim cried and the sandstorm beat on our shelter, howling in frustration at our escape.

It wasn't long before the boisterous wind calmed. I listened to the quiet until Kim said, "You're squashing me."

I backed out of the shelter. Kim rolled out after me, her black hair grayed by fine sand. I stood up in an alien world as smooth as frosting. I stared around me in surprise. It was beautiful. Kim bumped into my pack. "Hey, Kim, how'd you get here?" I asked. Kim took so long rubbing her fingers through her hair that I figured she was avoiding the question. "Kim?"

She flipped her gray hair. "You'll laugh at me."

"No I won't," I assured her.

Kim folded her arms, and a trickle of sand fell from her shirt to the ground. "I'm here because . . . because . . . I got tired of shopping."

I grinned. "That's great!"

"I got sick of carrying everything around, too," Kim admitted. "Once I got a little way down the trail, I just gave it all away. There was a place with a theater where I just dumped everything."

"I was at the theater," I said. "Did you meet Beatrice?"

Kim grinned. "Yeah. She really liked my shiny shirt."

The sun sat on the horizon, pointing with deep red rays to a sign that read, "This way."

"Hey!" I called. "Here's a sign!" Taking my bearings from the sun, I figured that the arrow pointed at where the huge dune once stood, but now the sand mountain was gone. Across the expanse, I spotted a band of dark green.

Trees.

I whooped and hollered in delight. "Kim, look! Trees! Let's go," I yelled.

Kim looked up and squinted in the direction my arm waved. "Why are you going over there?" she asked.

"The sign says to."

"There was a sandstorm," Kim said patiently. "The sign could be all turned around."

I thumped it with my hand. "It feels solid."

"I don't believe it," Kim said. She eyed the line of trees. "It's dark in there." She twisted a strand of her dusty hair. "Those are probably mean monkey trees."

"Mean monkey trees?" I repeated, not sure I heard her right.

"Yeah," Kim said. "Just the kind of place where monkeys throw coconuts on your head before they jump down and bite you."

I was dumbstruck. Here she stood in barren sand with night coming on while distant trees offered shelter. Besides, there was a sign telling her to go toward the tree line. How could she even wonder if it was the right thing to do?

"Kim," I said at last. "I've never heard of mean monkey trees. And the sign says to go that way." I pointed. "We can protect each other."

"Even if they aren't mean monkey trees, I'm not sure that's what the sign means." Kim rubbed her arms, which created little waterfalls of sand. "It could be interpreted so many different ways."

I threw up my hands. "Are you serious?"

Kim looked at me as if I were dense. "Yes. I wouldn't kid about this. I can't believe how difficult this journey has been." She bent over and shook her hair, rubbing her scalp with her fingers again. "I hate all this sand!"

When she straightened, I said, "But you got to ride a boat across the lake."

Her eyes flashed. "You think that was easy?"

"It looked easy from where I was treading water."

"Just because something looks easy doesn't mean it is. You can't judge unless you've done it yourself. I had to drive that boat alone, I had to start it up, navigate, watch for hazards, and keep it on course. It was so stressful. I almost crashed into a boat with a boy in it." She shuddered and pressed her hands over her heart. "It was so scary. I don't know how I missed him. He was down so low in the water that if he hadn't thrown a rock at the wheelhouse, it would have been too late for sure."

"Okay," I said, "Forget the boat ride. What's so hard to understand about this sign? It says, 'This way' and there's even an arrow." I raised my arm and pointed to the band of green trees.

"That's from where you stand," Kim said. She circled the sign. "See? If I point from here," she stood to one side of the sign and sighted down her arm. "It would take me to a different spot in the trees."

"Only slightly,' I said. "You'd still be in the trees."

"But what if I were to miss something important by entering the trees at that point?" Kim asked. "I want to be sure."

"Sometimes you just have to have faith."

Kim sat down on the small shelter and repeated, "I want to be sure. There might be snakes or wild animals waiting to eat you up in there. Besides, what if another sandstorm comes along before reaching the trees? At least I have shelter here."

"Kim, the sandstorm blew away the huge sand dune so we could get to the trees easier."

"How do you know?"

I shook my head and dribbles of sand pelted my shoulders. "Because I feel it inside," I said. "I can't explain it any better than that."

"So you can't prove it," she said.

"Look, the dune is gone, isn't it?" I said, throwing my hands up. "You must have seen it before the storm."

"I saw it," Kim said. "I was deciding what to do about it when the storm came. It was awful. Everything's been awful. This whole journey is just too hard. I wish I'd stayed on the hill."

"Don't you want to reach the estate?"

"Not if it's this hard."

"Come on, Kim, let's go to the trees," I pleaded. "It will be dark really soon."

"Don't rush me," Kim said. "I don't care about night. I have a flashlight." She hugged herself and looked back toward the scarred mountain. "I could go back over on the tram. Derrick told Megan about a place that's green and comfortable."

"Kim, it's green and comfortable over there," I insisted, pointing at the trees for the third time. "If we go that way, things will get better."

"That's what I thought about the rock path," Kim said, folding her arms. "It looked so nice in those trees, and then, bam, rocks everywhere. I tried pushing the rake upside down ahead of me for awhile, but I got blisters." Kim held up her hands, but the fading sunlight was behind her and it was hard to see her palms. "When I saw Megan sprain her wrist, I turned around and went another way."

"But she kept going," I said.

"I'm not going to sit here the rest of my life," Kim said, her eyes blazing. "I'm going somewhere."

"There's not much time," I said.

"I just need to decide what to do," Kim said, crossing her arms.

"I really want you to come with me," I said.

"Maybe I will," Kim answered.

"But I don't want to wait," I said.

"Then go on," Kim stared straight ahead. "No one's stopping you."

She was right. I was only stopping myself, and coaxing her was using up valuable time. But I wanted so badly for her to come with me. "Are you sure?" I asked, afraid of her answer.

"Sure," Kim said. "If I end up staying the night, I'll sleep in the shelter and block the doorway with my backpack."

I stared at Kim for a moment. Part of me wanted to scream, call her names, and force her to go with me. But that wouldn't make anything better. So I bent over and gave her a hug. "Take care," I said, meaning it.

She patted my shoulder. "You, too."

I turned and took off running. My toes barely made a dent in the packed sand. I kept my eyes on the tree line as I hurried to beat the sunset.

CHAPTER 15

Reaching the tree line, I bent over with hands on knees, breathing hard, sneaker toes tapping the ground from the ends of the laces I still held. Dim light filtered through the leaves, showing no sign of the estate. Had anyone reached it yet? I wondered who might be seated on the mansion veranda, eating ice cream while watching the same beautiful sunset that dogged my heels and threatened to leave me in darkness.

I pulled on socks and shoes and began a slow jog through the dark green corridor. Several hundred yards further the path grew darker, but not from decreasing sunlight. Mud sucked at my shoes, trying to pull them off as I hurried faster, veering toward the edge of the path I hoped would be drier.

Suddenly, my feet lost firm ground and I foundered, sinking into a broth of mud and water. At first I was confused, then terrified, as scenes from old jungle movies flooded my mind. Quicksand. I whipped my head desperately from side to side, but there were no convenient vines trailing in the muck. I couldn't see anyone nearby to throw me a branch, either. I was a goner before I'd even finished my journey. What was the use? The sun was nearly down and my strength was gone. It would surely be easier to just give up.

But just as quickly as the thought came, it was pushed out by a sudden resolve welling up in me to do all I could to escape this quagmire. If I died trying, at least I would have done all I could. My first impulse was to thrash, scream, and lash out at the suffocating substance around me.

Swim.

Swim? Yes, that was it! Swimming was the best way to get free of this sucking substance that was mostly water. It was difficult to make myself lower my face closer to the muck. I had to pull my arms through the runny mud a couple of times before I got the courage to tip my body forward and kick my legs. It was like trying to swim through oatmeal. The drag on my limbs was incredibly strong. It would have been easier to sink into the thick goop than to fight it, but I refused to stop pulling and kicking my slow way through.

When I was almost ready to give up, I noticed a sign next to a huge green willow tree ahead. The branches arched out away from the trunk and dove downward, skimming the ground and forming a canopy over a path. The trail appeared to be solid, but then, so had the quicksand. I was too far away to read the words, but just now I didn't really care what it said. I was sick of signs. My muscles burned, my shoulders ached, and my legs protested.

Why had this journey been so hard? I had tried my best, but it seemed nothing had gone right. Perhaps the glorious estate we'd seen from the distant hilltop was nothing but a cardboard cutout that had been folded up and put away. Perhaps I was fighting for a life that wasn't worth this much struggle. Yet every time I thought I couldn't take another stroke, some hidden strength pushed me forward.

At last I reached the waiting branches and took a desperate grab, getting a handful of supple limbs. I hung on, swaying in the muck for a moment, letting euphoria spread through me. Then I pulled, using the willow as a climber's rope to work my way up onto the path. As soon as my feet found solid ground, I let go of the willow and bent to rest slippery hands on muddy knees. When my breath eased enough to let my eyes focus, I turned my head to read the sign. In the deepening dusk, I read, "You made it."

I made it! I collapsed onto the ground in tears, my soul filled with relief.

Then I heard a sound on the far side of the bog. When I turned, I was amazed to see Alex thrashing in the mire. I stared at him. "Alex?" He didn't answer. He was too busy sinking. Jumping to my feet, I yelled, "Swim!" My heart beat hard, desperate for Alex to make it through the quicksand. "It's safe over here!" I called. "Hurry! Grab onto the tree!"

Alex thrashed and sputtered, sinking, then thrashed again. I couldn't stop the tears from welling up and rolling down my face as he took quick stabs at the muck.

There was another splash behind him. Megan! Her bandaged arm disappeared in the quagmire, and her red head dipped under the slippery mud.

I couldn't stand it. I had to help them, even if it meant going back into the quicksand myself. I took a step toward my companions. A hand descended on my shoulder. Whirling around, I came face to face with our host. He watched my struggling friends with gentle compassion.

"We've got to help them," I cried.

He turned his eyes on me. "It won't help to pull them out when they aren't ready."

"But I made it!"

"You followed the signs, so you had enough strength to get through."

"What difference does that make?" I shouted, feeling no joy in my accomplishment if it meant watching others drown. "We can't let them die. We've got to help." I waded into the quicksand. When it reached my ankles, he took hold of me again.

"You don't break a chick's egg when it's trying to hatch or it won't survive," he said in a voice gentle with love.

I let out a little sob.

"Don't worry, Casey," our host said, his voice deep and comforting. "There are different paths to the estate. Some of them don't even have quicksand. I've opened the doors for everyone, but I won't force them through." He led me out of the quicksand, stopping when my soggy sneakers were on firm ground. "There are those who even find a place along the way where they are content to remain. If they ever want to move on, they are free to do it. And if it gets hard, I'm always ready to help, just as I helped you."

Confused, I looked up into his eyes. How had he helped me? He hadn't even been around since early this morning when he'd given me a pack and sent me on my merry, treacherous way.

But as I searched his face, I suddenly remembered the whispers I'd heard along the trail. I remembered how my feet picked up speed when I took the first step past the sign that said, "Climb," carrying me up the first part of the mountain. I had to finish the climb on my own to build up enough strength for the quicksand.

"Was this whole journey and training ground for this last bit?" I asked, jabbing a thumb at the quagmire.

"Think about what else I helped you with," he said gently. I remembered the urge to test the steadiness of Derrick's "This way," sign in the canyon, and the huge sand dune that was miraculously blown away in the storm.

Tears blurred my eyes. "Will you help Derrick?" I asked. "And Kim?"

"As much as they'll let me." His voice was infinitely kind. I closed my eyes and leaned my head against the tree trunk. "Casey, this isn't a race." I looked up at him with startled eyes. He grinned, then added, "Everyone's journey is different. Some take a lot longer than others, but everyone will be taken care of in the end. It's time for you to go on."

"I'm too tired."

Our host gave me an incredibly loving gaze, his chestnut hair burnished by the sun's final glow. "You're already there."

Surprised, I turned and saw the ornate gates not more than thirty paces from where I stood. Relief and gratitude washed through me, nearly making my knees buckle. "Thank you," I said, taking his hand and pressing it to my cheek.

"You're welcome, Casey," he said. "I love you."

I knew without a doubt that he did. I turned and moved along the trail, the joy in my heart lifting one foot and placing it before another. As I walked, the dirt turned into soft, spongy blacktop that gave my tired feet a little spring with each step. When I reached the gates, I couldn't help but look behind me. From the faint light fading behind the mountain, I made out our host on the far side of the quicksand, wrapping a blanket around Megan's shoulders while Alex crawled up onto the near shore by the willow tree.

"Alex!" I screamed. "You made it!"

Alex looked up at me and gave me a wink. Then he unzipped his pack and pulled out his towel. "You go on, Casey," he called. "I'll meet you there."

"Okay!" I yelled. He gave me a wave. I waved back. He rubbed his hair with the towel as I turned to the gates. I put my hand on one of them and pushed. It swung open and I stepped inside.

Up close, everything on the estate was more beautiful than I had imagined. The mansion was lit with bright lights against the night, glowing in gentle majesty. The waterfall sang a cheerful cadence, sparkling in a spotlight that polished each water drop to brilliance. The flowers turned their sleepy faces toward me in welcome. Even though I still wore my sodden sneakers, the grass was like velvet under my feet. I was happy just to stand there. But the setting sun left me chilled, reminding me that I was wearing wet, muddy clothes. Besides that, I was hungry.

Someone moved toward me along a manicured walk. When I looked to see who it was, I could hardly believe my eyes. What kind of trick was this? The blonde boy who was so fond of throwing rocks stopped and stared back at me, his eyes wide with surprise. I raised my hands in self-defense and asked, "What are you doing here?"

"A man told me to come."

"What man?"

"The nice man in the plaid shirt and blue jeans."

"Impossible," I said. "You threw rocks at me."

"I don't have any rocks now," the boy mumbled.

"But why are you here?" I asked. "This is supposed to be my reward, the end of my long, hard journey."

"Mine, too."

My mouth fell open. "No way."

The boy lowered his eyes for an instant, then looked at me again. "I didn't say I did everything right. I just did the best I could. You weren't perfect, either, you know."

"But I followed the signs!"

"Remember all your doubts, the time you wasted making decisions when you already knew what to do, the grumbling about how hard it was instead of being grateful that you could walk?"

I folded my arms. "At least I didn't throw rocks at anybody."

The boy raised his shoulders and let them down again. "My path was different than yours."

Suddenly, my stomach rumbled. "I'm supposed to get dinner here," I announced, hoping to cover up the noise.

He shook his head. "I don't know where any is." Then he gazed at me with hopeful eyes. "Maybe if we go inside we'll find some moldy bread and a rotten apple."

My heart softened at his words. I relaxed and gave him a smile. "Come on," I said, then started toward the front of the mansion.

"You really want me to go with you?"

I stopped and turned around. "Sure."

"Why?"

I shrugged. "Why not?"

"Because . . . because," it seemed the words stuck in his throat, but finally he said, "I was mean to you."

"You're not mean now."

He blinked several times. "You see, it's just that so many people were mean to me that I decided to be mean first so it wouldn't hurt as bad. But the man in the blue jeans, Jesus, told me that's not how it works. He said now that I know better, I need to make different choices. If I do all I can, that's good enough for him. So I'm telling you I'm sorry, because I really am." The boy stared at his feet. "Please don't be mad at me."

A gentle thought brushed my mind. Heed the signs.

"It's okay," I said my heart unexpectedly brimming over with love for this boy with the stubborn cowlick on the side of his head. "Hey, what's your name? It's not Rock Boy, is it?"

The boy flashed his eyes up at me. Seeing my grin, he smiled back and shook his head. "Jesus called me The Least of These."

"The Least of These?"

"Yeah. When some guys were chasing me with clubs, he stopped them and said that whatever's done to the least of these is done to him." The boy's grin broadened. "He meant me!"

I laughed, moved closer, and slid my arm around his shoulder. In spite of the crusted mud on my clothes, the boy didn't hesitate to wrap his arms around me and give me a big hug right back.

"Know what?" he said. "You're The Least of These, too."

And I knew that I was.

ABOUT THE AUTHOR

Shirley Anderson Bahlmann has loved reading and writing since she was a child. She believes that stories are magic because they never wear out!

Shirley's versatile style has seen her write everything from true stories to novels to a children's book with instructions on how to roll your own chicken!

You can email Shirley at:

yoshirley@yahoo.com

or visit her website at:

www.thebestandfunniestever.com

Thank you for reading!

Made in the USA
Charleston, SC
23 March 2014